THE LYLE ANTIQUES & THEIR VALUES

GLASS

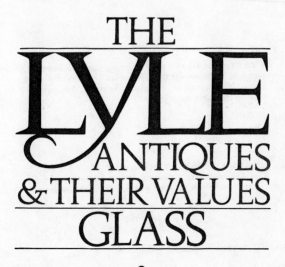

THE LYLE ANTIQUES & THEIR VALUES GLASS

•

Compiled by Anthony Curtis

While every care has been taken in the compiling of information contained in this volume the publishers cannot accept any liability for loss, financial or otherwise, incurred by reliance placed on the information herein.

All prices quoted in this book are obtained from a variety of auctions in various countries and are converted to dollars at the rate of exchange prevalent at the time of sale.

Library of Congress Cataloging in Publication Data

Curtis, Tony.
  Glass.

  (Antiques and their values)
  Includes index.
  1. Glassware—Collectors and collecting—Catalogs.
2. Glassware—Prices. I. Title. II. Series: Curtis,
Tony. Antiques and their values.
NK5105.C87 1982   748.2'075   82-1479
ISBN 0-698-11159-1   AACR2

Printed in the United States of America
Distributed in the United States by Coward, McCann & Geoghegan,
200 Madison Avenue, New York, N.Y. 10016

INTRODUCTION

This book is one of a series specially devised to aid the busy professional dealer in his everyday trading. It will also prove to be of great value to all collectors and those with goods to sell, for it is crammed with illustrations, brief descriptions and valuations of hundreds of antiques.

Every effort has been made to ensure that each specialised volume contains the widest possible variety of goods in its particular category though the greatest emphasis is placed on the middle bracket of trade goods rather than on those once-in-a-lifetime museum pieces whose values are of academic rather than practical interest to the vast majority of dealers and collectors.

This policy has been followed as a direct consequence of requests from dealers who sensibly realise that, no matter how comprehensive their knowledge, there is always a need for reliable, up-to-date reference works for identification and valuation purposes.

When using your Antiques and their Values Book to assess the worth of goods, please bear in mind that it would be impossible to place upon any item a precise value which would hold good under all circumstances. No antique has an exactly calculable value; its price is always the result of a compromise reached between buyer and seller, and questions of condition, local demand and the business acumen of the parties involved in a sale are all factors which affect the assessment of an object's 'worth' in terms of hard cash.

In the final analysis, however, such factors cancel out when large numbers of sales are taken into account by an experienced valuer, and it is possible to arrive at a surprisingly accurate assessment of current values of antiques; an assessment which may be taken confidently to be a fair indication of the worth of an object and which provides a reliable basis for negotiation.

Throughout this book, objects are grouped under category headings and, to expedite reference, they progress in price order within their own categories. Where the description states 'one of a pair' the value given is that for the pair sold as such.

CONTENTS

GLASS

ALE GLASSES

Pressed ale glass with simulated capstan stem, circa 1870. $15

U bowl ale glass with arch molded decoration and knopped stem, circa 1840. $30

Capstan stemmed ale glass with arch decoration, circa 1840. $35

U bowl ale with molded cut thumbprint decoration, circa 1850. $35

Short ale glass with wrythen decoration, 4½ ins. high, circa 1860. $35

U bowl ale glass engraved with hops and barley, circa 1840. $40

Short ale glass with lemon squeezer foot, circa 1800. $40

Late 18th century hop and barley engraved ale glass. $40

Engraved plain stemmed ale glass of Jacobite significance, circa 1750, 18cm. high. $140

GLASS

Engraved plain stemmed ale glass with funnel bowl, circa 1745, 18cm. high. $170

Facet-stemmed ale glass with slender funnel bowl, circa 1780, 16cm. high. $170

Cotton twist ale glass, circa 1770. $180

Opaque twist ale glass with slender ogee bowl, circa 1770, 19.5cm. high. $207

Unusual cut ale wine glass, 7in. high, circa 1770. $225

Air twist ale glass with slender funnel bowl, circa 1750, 20.5cm. high. $255

Engraved air twist ale glass of drawn trumpet shape, circa 1770, 19.5cm. high. $255

Dwarf ale glass, circa 1750, 4in. high, bowl with wry-then molding . $270

Air twist ale glass, with round funnel bowl engraved with a single hop and two leaves, 1750, 19.7cm. high. $300

9

ALE GLASSES

Mixed twist ale glass with a plain conical foot, 1770, 19.1cm. high. $325

Opaque twist ale glass with tall round funnel bowl, 1760. $345

Engraved ale glass with tall ogee bowl, circa 1765, 7in. high. $360

English opaque twist ale glass. $360

Engraved air twist ale glass with two ears of barley, circa 1750, 19cm. high. $390

An ale glass, 8in. high, circa 1750. $400

Ale glass with round funnel bowl finely engraved with hops and barley, circa 1750, 8¼in. high. $405

Balustroid engraved ale glass with slender funnel bowl, circa 1740, 18cm. high. $440

Short Wrythen ale glass with funnel bowl, circa 1730, 5½in. high. $525

GLASS

A Jacobite ale glass with tall bell bowl, circa 1750, 8in. high. $620

An engraved Jacobite ale glass with air twist stem. $630

Baluster stem ale glass with triple knop above an inverted baluster, circa 1740. $630

A double knopped air twist ale glass, circa 1760. $725

Engraved ale glass, 6,1/8 ins. high, circa 1760. $750

Baluster ale glass with straight-sided funnel bowl, circa 1700, 18cm. high. $800

Fine early ale glass with conical bowl, circa 1700, 5½in. high. $950

Anglo-Venetian ale glass, 6in. high, circa 1690. $1,295

Rare canary yellow color twist ale glass. $1,950

GLASS

APOTHECARY BOXES

Mahogany apothecary box complete with bottles, circa 1820.
$190

A mahogany apothecary cabinet with a secret poison compartment, twenty-six assorted bottles, and brass scales, circa 1790 $240

Late 18th century mahogany apothecary box complete with the original bottles.
$270

19th century homeo-pathic medicine chest with twenty-four glass bottles, circa 1870, 9in. long. $420

Early 19th century mahogany chemist's chest complete with fittings. $495

George III shagreen cased apothecary's chest, circa 1760.
$530

Early 19th century English apothecary's chest, 8in. high.
$640

Late Georgian mahogany apothe-cary's cabinet, 9½in. high.
$650

English A. S. Maw & Sons portable medical cabinet, circa 1863, 6½in. high.
$675

GLASS

Georgian apothecary's box in mahogany with fitted drawer, circa 1810. $735

Brass bound George III mahogany apothecary's box by Cox & Robinson. $765

Early 19th century English apothecary's chest in mahogany, 23cm. wide, closed. $950

Georgian mahogany and brass bound apothecary's box, complete with bottles. $965

Mahogany 'Duke of York' apothecary cabinet, circa 1780. $1,040

Mid 19th century English double-sided apothecary's chest in mahogany case, 23cm. wide. $1,055

Outstanding George III mahogany apothecary cabinet on bracket feet, with old bottles, pestle and mortar, 15in. circa 1795. $1,155

George III mahogany apothecary cabinet by Paytherus, Savory & Moore. $1,215

Early 19th century English apothecary's cabinet, 15in. high. $1,575

13

GLASS

BASKETS

Late Victorian light blue slag glass basket. $35

A Sowerby's of Gateshead 'blanc de lait', slag glass ornamental basket, 8 cm. wide. $35

Victorian silver sugar basket with a blue glass liner, London, 1846, 5 oz. $170

Late 19th century amberina glass overshot basket with a looped handle, 12.5cm. high. $325

Tiffany bronze and gold iridescent bride's basket, 7½in. high. $485

Cameo glass bride's basket by Mount Washington Glass Co. $765

BEERSTEINS

An Imperial German cut glass half litre beerstein with a heavily plated lid surmounted by a Jaeger shako. $65

A fine Imperial German glass, half litre beerstein. $125

A good Imperial German Reservist's glass, half litre beerstein, painted with the Kaiser's portrait. $150

14

Newcastle purple and white slag glass beaker. $35

Late 19th century Venetian-style mauve glass beaker with white glass decoration. $35

19th century Mary Gregory beaker depicting a young girl. $90

Lead glass beaker with an oval medallion, showing a square rigged sailing ship and 'Grove Hill', 6¾ ins. high. $135

18th century German enameled glass beaker of tapered cylindrical form, 3¼in. high. $200

A fine English beaker engraved with a church, a mill and a fort flying the Union Jack, circa 1760. $200

Saxon-engraved glass beaker of bell shape, circa 1745, 10.5cm. high. $275

Bohemian beaker with waisted cylindrical body, frosted overall with gilt rim, circa 1835, 11.5cm. high. $315

Small engraved Nuremberg beaker and cover, early 18th century, 4¾in. high. $340

BEAKERS

Pale bluish green glass beaker on hollow folded pad foot, 3rd-4th century A.D., 3¼in. high. $340

Late 18th century Bohemian double overlay beaker. $345

Pale green glass beaker with slightly convex sides, 1st-2nd century A.D., 2½in. high. $360

Unusual amber-flashed beaker of thistle form, circa 1850, 16.2cm. high. $395

Pale yellowish green glass beaker with straight flaring sides, circa 3rd century A.D., 3¼in. high. $405

One of a pair of Silesian engraved fluted beakers with minor chips, 4¼in. high, circa 1755. $410

Small German beaker, enameled with a flower, dated 1721, 7cm. high. $420

Engraved beaker of cylindrical form with everted rim, circa 1820, 9.5cm. high. $475

German glass beaker engraved with hunting scenes. $540

Lithyalin beaker of cylindrical slightly flared section, circa 1830, 11.4cm. high. $630

Bohemian overlay beaker enameled with hunting scenes, circa 1850, 14.8cm. high. $805

Bohemian ruby glass gilt and enameled spa beaker, circa 1840, 12cm. high. $825

Thuringian dated armorial beaker with bell bowl, 1733, 12cm. high. $875

Bohemian enameled overlay beaker with flared bowl, circa 1840, 12.5cm. high. $900

Silesian engraved beaker with ogee bowl, circa 1760, 11.5cm. high. $910

One of a pair of Bohemian overlay gilt and enameled beakers, circa 1840, 12cm. high. $1,000

Good Bohemain engraved beaker, circa 1830, 13.8cm. high. $1,035

Rare St. Louis millefiori beaker, 10cm. high. $1,035

GLASS

BEAKERS

An opaque white glass beaker enameled in colors, 9 cm. $1,045

Unusual 18th century Spanish tumbler, 12cm. high. $1,065

Venetian enameled tumbler, 18th century, 4½in. high. $1,210

Facon de Venise flared beaker, 16th/17th century, 6in. high. $1,240

German beaker on three hollow ball feet, engraved with Imperial Arms and artisans' emblems, circa 1730, 10.5cm. high. $1,240

German engraved armorial beaker, circa 1740, 12cm. high. $1,440

Silesian footed beaker engraved in Tiefschnitt, 5½in. high, circa 1730. $1,520

Mid 19th century Bohemian amber flash transparentemail beaker with waisted bowl, 13cm. high. $1,595

A beaker of grey Lithyalin glass by Freidrich Egermann of Blottendorf, 13ins. high, first half of 19th century. $1,725

18th century enameled Bohemian beaker, 4in. high. $1,765

18th century enameled German beaker, 7in. high. $1,765

A fine amber colored beaker signed Anton Kothgasser (1769-1851). $2,160

Bohemian flared beaker in white glass, 12cm. high. $2,195

Landscape beaker from the Mohn workshop, circa 1815, 4½ in. $2,235

Rare German beaker, 16th/17th century, 4½in. high. $2,250

Gilt and 'Transparentemail' Ranftbecher by Anton Kothgasser, circa 1820, 11cm. high. $2,700

Glass Facon de Venise beaker. $4,050

Bohemian Royal Portrait armorial beaker and cover, early 18th century, 19.5cm. high. $4,290

19

BEAKERS

A deep-colored marbled glass beaker by F. Egermann, 4¼in. high. $4,920

North Bohemian lithyalin flared beaker by F. Egermann, circa 1830, 13.5cm. high. $5,625

Early 19th century enameled glass beaker decorated by Anton Kothgasser, 12cm. $6,485

Late 17th century wheel-engraved ruby glass beaker, South German, 12.5 cm. $8,250

Glass beaker with enameled band of flowers by Mohn Jnr., 4½ in. $8,310

One of a pair of egg-yolk yellow Pekin glass beakers, 9½in. high. $10,685

Transparent enameled beaker from the workshop of Samuel Mohn, 1812, 9.8cm. high. $18,000

Venetian enameled beaker, circa 1520, 8¾in. high. $54,000

Dated Elizabethan engraved inscription beaker. $185,000

BEILBY WINE GLASSES

A Beilby ogee bowl wine glass, 5¼in. high. $520

Beilby wine glass with conical bowl enameled in white, 1780, 15.2 cm. high. $575

Beilby wine glass with ogee bowl enameled in white with a band of baroque rococo scrolling, 1770, 15.2cm. high. $755

A Beilby ale glass decorated with barley hops in white enamel. $875

Beilby enameled glass with bell bowl, 6½in. high, circa 1765. $1,135

Beilby enameled glass, circa 1770, 6in. high, with ogee bowl. $1,285

A rare Beilby enameled Masonic glass. $1,440

Beilby enameled wine glass with gilded rim, 1770, 17.4cm. high. $1,530

A Beilby wine glass with a flared round funnel bowl decorated with a landscape scene in colored enamel. $1,550

21

GLASS

BELLS

Nailsea bell of red and blue mottled covering on a white ground. $270

Latticinio bell mounted in silver gilt, circa 1600, 9½in. high. $4,500

Late 16th century silver mounted latticinio bell, 5½in. high. $6,300

BISCUIT CONTAINERS

Victorian circular cut glass biscuit jar with a plated stand and cover. $45

Late 19th century glass biscuit barrel with plated mounts. $45

Victorian engraved glass biscuit jar on a plated and engraved stand with bun feet. $65

BOOKENDS

One of a pair of frosted glass bookends in the form of elephants, signed J. Hoffman, 14cm. high. $170

Pair of Lalique glass bookends, engraved 'R. Lalique', 1920's, 19.25cm. high. $1,640

Pair of Walter pate de verre bookends, 1920's, 17cm. high. $3,715

Brown glass beer
bottle. $5

Sheared-top sauce bottle
of green tinted glass. $5

Small mineral water bottle.
                    $5

Bung-stoppered mineral
water bottle. $9

Amber glass hair tonic
bottle. $9

Early 20th century one
pint brown glass beer
bottle with screw-in
stopper. $10

Victorian poison bottle
marked 'Not To Be Taken',
8in. high. $12

Victorian baby's feeding
bottle. $14

German mineral water
bottle in dark green
glass. $14

BOTTLES

'Dumpy' green glass safecure bottle for diabetics. $18

Early 20th century blue syphon bottle. $22

Clarke's clear fluid ammonia bottle. $24

Cobalt blue bottle marked 'Poison' $30

Four Victorian green fluted glass medicine bottles and stoppers, 24cm. high. $30

Red glass Barrel Bitters bottle, American, circa 1860-80, 9¼in. high. $40

Codd's glass mineral bottle with amber stopper. $40

Opaque, deep blue glass decanter bottle by Mowart of Scotland, circa 1920. $45

Birdcage ink bottle on square base, in pale green glass, 3¼in. high, circa 1860-90. $50

Amber glass Indian Queen Bitters bottle, circa 1870-80, 12¼in. high. $50

Pair of sealed sherry bottles, 'Dry Sack, Williams and Humber', circa 1880. $75

Gigantic green glass bottle, mid 17th century, 15in. high. $90

Early 19th century Zara Seal liqueur bottle with ring-postil base.$100

Daffy's Elixir Cure All bottle. $100

A blown and molded sealed bottle dated 1802. $110

Codd's amber glass mineral bottle. $110

Á large globular purple chemist's bottle with stopper and gilt and black "Syr. Phos. C." label, 14ins. high. $110

Price's Patent Candle Co. cough medicine bottle in cobalt blue glass. $110

BOTTLES

Small, 18th century, iridescent bottle of mallet form.
$115

A Bristol blue glass ket-
chip bottle. $120

One of a pair of Georgian
silver and glass condiment
bottles, 1808, 7in. high.
$125

Green blown glass bottle
with etched decoration and
dated 1829, 30cm. high.
$125

Pear-shaped chemist's shop
window display drug bottle,
18in. high, 19th century.
$145

Warner's green glass
safecure bottle for
diabetics. $145

One of a pair of 18th
century green glass
spirit bottles, 11½in.
high. $150

Rare bitters bottle dated
1874. $160

One of a pair of Bohemian
ruby glass bottles and stoppers, circa 1850, 24.5cm.
high. $170

One of a pair of small Bristol blue colored sauce bottles with lozenge stoppers, 6in. $180

An Oxford tavern bottle dated 1684. $180

Mid 19th century pressed amber glass Bitters bottle by A. M. Bininger & Co., 32cm. high. $180

One of three spirit bottles and stoppers, possibly Cork glass, 16.5cm. high. $200

An English sealed wine bottle, the seal showing a comet with five trailing rays, indicating the comet year 1811, 12¾ in. high. $210

Egyptian graveware tear bottle. $210

19th century chemist's clear glass shop sign, circa 1850, 26in. high. $235

Dutch spirit bottle, 6in. tall. $250

Victorian satin glass bottle, 7½in. high. $270

BOTTLES

American blown three-mold bottle in olive green glass, circa 1830, 17cm. high. $275

Heavily swirled glass brandy bar bottle in emerald green, 27.5cm. high, circa 1840-60. $290

Sealed wine bottle of dark brown metal, 8¼in. high, 1736. $300

Enameled bottle, circa 1870, 11.8cm. high, with gilt rim. $325

Sealed wine bottle, dark olive green, with kick-in base, circa 1765, 24cm. high. $340

Early 19th century American blown three-mold aqua bottle, 21cm. high. $350

H. Codd's cobalt blue marble stoppered bottle. $360

Sealed wine bottle, 1742, 9¼in. high. $395

19th century Nailsea bottle, 8in. high. $420

GLASS

One of a pair of pressed glass bar bottles with flared bases, Sandwich, Massachusetts, 10in. high, circa 1850. $425

Serving bottle, dark olive green with opaque white inclusions, Shropshire, circa 1800, 12.5cm. high. $430

Rare early wine bottle, circa 1660, 8in. high. $430

Small 18th century Sang-de-Boeuf bottle, 4¾in. high. $450

Early English dark green wine bottle, circa 1680, 7¾in. high. $485

French blown-in mold Pocahontas bottle, circa 1830, 2 x 2¼in. $500

Sealed wine bottle, 8¼in. high, circa 1730. $510

Hand-painted Egyptian bottle, 400 B.C. $570

Late 17th century sealed bottle of heavy green metal, 7in. high. $570

BOTTLES

Sealed wine bottle, inscribed O R Bury, 1763, 7½in. high.
$595

German enameled pharmacy bottle, circa 1740, 9.5cm. high. $600

Late 17th century squat dark green wine bottle, 16cm. high. $600

Early sealed wine bottle, seal inscribed 'Robt. Tanner 1725', 8¾in. high.
$620

Attractive Pekin glass bottle of transparent amber colored metal, Qianlong period, 20.3cm. high.
$675

Late 19th century English carboy, one of a pair, on wooden base, 107cm. high.
$715

Sealed and dated wine bottle inscribed Saml. Whittuck, 1751, 9in. high. $735

One of a set of four gilt toilet bottles, 20cm. high, circa 1830, with matching stoppers. $785

Serving bottle with globular body and slender tapering neck, circa 1730, 19.5cm. high. $820

Large pale green glass bottle with indented base, circa 14th century A.D., 15½in. high.$900

Blown-in mold bottle in green color, New England, circa 1825, 6¼in. high. $900

Sealed wine bottle with short tapering cylindrical neck, 7in. high, circa 1725. $970

Early English dark green wine bottle, circa 1660, 9½in. high. $1,035

Two from a set of six etched and cut glass spirit bottles, circa 1840. $1,125

Good red overlay Pekin glass bottle, with decoration of birds in flowering prunus trees, circa 1800, 19.1cm. high. $1,305

Quezal iridescent glass and silver overlay bottle, inscribed Quezal, 22.5cm. high.$1,320

Sealed and dated wine bottle of dark green metal, inscribed W. Skammell, 1704, 6in. high. $1,345

Rare Pekin glass double gourd bottle, clear pink flecked metal with blue overlay, 18th century, 15.5cm. high.$1,350

31

BOTTLES

Unusually large early
sealed wine bottle,
10in. high, circa 1728..
$1,375

German 18th century ena-
meled apothecary bottle,
4¾in. high. $1,400

Sealed wine bottle
of onion shape, 1705,
6¾in. high. $1,440

Iridescent cobalt blue
bottle by Loetz with tall
tapering neck, 28.5cm.
high. $1,560

1st century A.D. small blue
glass bottle with squat pear-
shaped body, 3in. high.
$1,575

Bohemian Zwischengold
bottle with silver cap, 12cm.
high. $1,575

Dark green sealed wine
bottle, inscribed John
Luke, 1721. $1,620

Sealed and dated wine
bottle, inscribed I. Smith,
1706, 6¾in. high.
$1,690

Early sealed wine bottle,
5¼in. high, circa 1712.
$1,835

Early sealed wine bottle, circa 1683, 6in. high. $1,845

Netherlandish blue glass bottle. $1,890

Rare Sidonian bottle, circa 100 A.D. $2,160

Nuremberg wheel engraved glass bottle, circa 1720, 27cm. high. $2,250

Rare early tavern bottle of strong green metal, 1684, 6in. high. $3,330

Rare and unrecorded early sealed wine bottle, 7¼in. high, circa 1670. $4,275

Rare overlay oviform bottle and stopper, signed, 8¾in. high. $5,795

Tiffany green ground bottle, circa 1905. $6,190

Leyden, Netherlands green tinted glass bottle, 28cm. high. $21,350

33

GLASS

BOWLS

Edwardian pressed glass
sugar bowl. $9

A small pressed blue
glass Victorian dressing
table bowl and cover,
3in. diam. $15

Victorian mauve carnival
glass bowl. $22

Victorian white slag glass
bowl with thistle decora-
tion. $35

Decorative Victorian
glass bowl. $30

Victorian ruby glass bowl,
6in. diam. $35

Milk glass crimped bowl.
          $35

19th century French glass
bowl with enameled deco-
ration, 8in. wide. $90

Fine iridescent Art Glass
bowl with wavy rim, 10in.
diam. $105

White glass sugar
bowl, possibly
made on Tyneside.
$125

Late 19th century frosted
glass bowl with applied
decoration and wavy rim.
$130

19th century **Lalique glass**
bowl of clear and opaque
white glass, 10in. diam.
$165

**Signed glass bowl by
Sabena, France.**
$170

Findlay onyx opalescent
covered sugar bowl, circa
1890, Ohio, 5¾in. high.
$175

Regency period glass
punchbowl, finely
engraved with grapes,
hops and barley, with
shield monogram H.M.M.
and dated 1806. $210

Powder bowl by Lalique
decorated with antelopes
in white glass, circa 1915.
$215

19th century Eastern
United States three-color
cut-glass bowl, 5in. diam.
$225

Lalique opalescent glass
'sirens' bowl, circa 1930,
20.75cm. diam. $350

BOWLS

A Georgian cut glass punchbowl and domed cover, on cut stem and square base, 17 in. $240

Lalique glass bowl with star-shaped fern design, signed, 35cm. diam. $250

A Waterford glass fruit bowl. $270

Opaque blue bowl and stand, circa 1850, 27.5cm. high. $285

Irish cut glass fruit bowl, 8in. diam., circa 1800. $295

Wheeling peach blow rose-bowl, 5½in. high. $300

Unusual clear green Pekin glass bowl, decorated in relief with birds and blossom, 16.2cm. diam. $340

Part of a late 19th century set of eighteen Venetian bowls and stands, 15.8cm. diam. $355

Portrait overlay footed bowl in ruby glass, circa 1850, 28cm. high. $365

Georgian cut glass punch-bowl and cover, on stand, circa 1820. $380

18th century Latticinio shallow bowl, probably Catalan, 18cm. diam. $385

Rare caddy bowl in cut blue glass, circa 1810. $395

Early 20th century iridescent glass bowl, marked Quezal, New York, 13cm. diam. $400

Northwood purple carnival glass punchbowl and stand with cups, Ohio, circa 1910, 10in. high. $400

Rare Lynn finger bowl of dark emerald green metal, circa 1765, 11.5cm. diam. $405

One of a set of three Tiffany iridescent glass finger bowls, circa 1900, 12cm. diam. $440

Hawkes cut-glass fruit bowl, Corning, New York, circa 1900, 12in. diam. $450

'L'Homme Lefevre de Caranza' lustre glass bowl, circa 1900, 7.5cm. wide. $450

BOWLS

Tiffany blue iridescent bowl with swirled blown out body. $450

Irish cut glass turnover bowl, 10in. diam., circa 1800. $460

A small Lalique bowl and cover of compressed form, 7cm. diam. $500

Large early 20th century Sinclaire & Co. intaglio cut fruit bowl, Corning, New York. $500

Glass boat shaped bowl with bayeuge cutting. $505

English cut glass orange bowl, 12in. wide, circa 1790. $520

A Lalique circular bowl and cover of matt glass with slightly flared sides, 8cm. diam. $520

Antique American brilliant-cut punchbowl, 34.6cm. diam. $530

A Galle cameo glass bowl, the pale pink body overlaid in green and etched with teasels, 19cm. wide. $540

Islamic green mould blown glass bowl, circa 10th century A.D., 6in. diam.
$540

Bristol finger bowl marked I. Jacobs, Bristol. $540

Pale bluish green cast glass 'pillar- molded' bowl, 1st century A.D., 4¼in. diam.
$585

Bronze mounted iridescent glass bowl, by Loetz, circa 1900, 23.5cm. high.
$585

Overlay footed bowl in ruby and white, on tall pedestal base, circa 1850, 34.8cm. high. $605

Galle cameo glass bowl and cover, circa 1900, 11cm. diam. $615

Miniature cameo glass bowl, circa 1880, 3.8cm. high. $615

16th century Venetian 'chalcedony' bowl with everted rim, 12.5cm. diam. $625

Glass bowl by Gabriel Argy Rousseau. $630

GLASS

BOWLS

Cameo glass bowl in frosted glass overlaid in pink and white, 1880's, 7.3cm. $675

Daum iron mounted glass bowl in red glass, signed, 10¼in. diam. $695

Rare blue overlay Pekin glass waterpot of translucent white metal, 18th century, 5.4cm. high. $825

Pekin glass bowl of clear carmine metal, decorated with dragons in relief, 19.7cm. wide.$850

Heavy Walter pate de verre stemmed bowl, 15cm. high, 1920's. $850

Clear yellow Pekin glass bowl, carved with fruit trees and bats, mark of Qianlong, 14.5cm. wide. $870

A Tiffany Favrile golden iridescent bowl with globular body, 19cm. high. $900

Palais Royale ormolu mounted translucent red bowl and cover, circa 1830, 16cm. high. $900

Galle enameled glass bowl, circa 1900, 16.25cm. diam. $985

Daum cameo glass bowl
with quatrefoil rim, circa
1900, 15.5cm. wide.
$990

Late 19th century Eastern
United States cut-glass
two-part punchbowl, 14in.
diam. $1,000

Good Irish canoe fruit
bowl, 14in. wide, circa
1810. $1,050

Galle cameo glass bowl,
marked, circa 1900, in
milky gray glass, 18.8cm.
diam. $1,075

Blue glass bowl with French
silver gilt mounts, circa
1825, 11½in. high.
$1,080

An Orrefors deep bowl by
Edvin Ohrstrom, 18cm.
diam. $1,080

Galle cameo glass bowl,
circa 1900, 11.5cm. wide.
$1,125

Orrefors engraved glass
bowl and plate, 1927,
38cm. long. $1,125

A Brocard enameled Mogul
jade bowl, 16.5cm. high.
$1,240

GLASS

BOWLS

Very rare double-walled bowl attributed to Thos. Hawkes, 4¼in. diam., circa 1830-37. $1,295

19th century Webb two-color cameo glass bowl, signed, 9½in. diam. $1,350

Galle etched and enameled glass bowl and cover, circa 1900, 19cm. high. $1,520

Green glass bowl, cover and stand, circa 1850, 31cm. high. $1,530

Early 20th century Irish brilliant cut-glass punch-bowl, sold with matching stand, 14¼in. high. $1,600

An early English glass covered bowl. $1,605

17th century Venetian glass bowl, 43cm. diam. $1,760

Early 19th century American expanding dip mold amber glass bowl, 20cm. diam. $1,900

German 'Maigerlein', 16th century, 4¼in. diam. $1,915

Large flared bowl stipple engraved by Laurence Whistler, 9¾in. diam. $2,080

Early 16th century Venetian bowl enameled in red and white, 6¼in. diameter. $2,400

A fine English cameo-cut bowl. $3,300

16th or 17th century Facon de Venise Latticinio shallow bowl, possibly Venetian, 13.5cm. diam. $4,950

Early 18th century glass bowl, 11¼in. diam. $9,900

Ravenscroft large glass bowl, 15½in. diam., circa 1674/82. $11,250

Fine quality bowl by Francois-Emile Decorchemont. $15,120

Bohemian 'Schwarzlot' covered bowl by Ignaz Preissler, 6¾in. high, circa 1725. $19,500

5th century B.C. Iranian pale green glass bowl, 6¾in. diam. $168,750

GLASS

BOXES

19th century ruby glass circular box and cover, 4in. $90

Lalique glass powder box and cover, circa 1925, 10.7cm. diam. $585

18kt. gold mounted clear glass powder box by Alfred Clark, 11.5cm. long, London, 1901. $1,585

BUGLES & HORNS

Bristol blue hunting horn, circa 1820. $120

One of a pair of blue glass bugles. $225

Rare internally decorated textured Galle glass horn, circa 1900, 42.5cm. long. $2,850

CADDIES

Victorian purple slag glass tea caddy of sarcophagus form. $170

Rare Staffordshire 'enamel' tea bottle, 5½in. high, circa 1760. $675

Rare enameled armorial rectangular tea caddy and stopper, 7in. high. $2,025

GLASS

CANDELABRA

A large ornate brass candlestick with crystal glass drops, 24½ in. high. $170

A pair of brass candelabra each for five lights with four branches, the bell shaped candleholders with wax pans and amber cut glass pear shaped drops, 23½ins. $630

One of a fine pair of French ormolu three branch candelabra with cut glass prism drops, 14 in. high, circa 1830. $630

One of a pair of Regency plaster, marble and glass candlesticks. $845

One of a pair of glass and gilt metal candelabra. $1,235

One of a pair of Lalique four-light candelabra, 9½in. high. $1,630

One of a pair of cut-glass two-light candelabra, circa 1780, 71cm. high. $3,360

Fine bronze and iridescent Favrile glass six-branched candelabrum by Tiffany, 15in. high. $4,500

One of a pair of Regency table lights with ormolu and glass bases, 30in. high. $7,200

45

GLASS

CANDLESTICKS

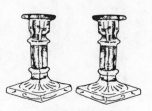

Edwardian molded glass candlestick. $9

Pair of 20th century molded glass candlesticks. $15

Victorian multi-colored glass candlestick. $27

Late 19th century glass candlestick, 10in. high. $27

Victorian ruby glass candlestick. $27

Art Deco red and clear glass candlestick. $36

Victorian cut-glass candlestick. $45

19th century purple slag glass candlestick. $45

Late 18th century candlestick with flat cut stem. $90

Silver lustre mercury glass candlestick. $100

Glass candlestick, cylindrical nozzle set on a domed and folded foot, 2¾in. high, circa 1720. $100

19th century Nailsea glass candlestick. $135

Richardson opal glass candlestick, circa 1850. $190

Freeblown glass candlestick, Massachusetts, circa 1860, 8½in. high. $220

Late 18th century free blown glass pricket candlestick, 9in. high. $290

One of a pair of Canary dolphin glass candlesticks, with petal rim cup, circa 1845, 25cm. high. $300

Silesian stemmed taperstick on octagonally molded stem, circa 1740, 13.5cm. high. $305

Small baluster taperstick on high terraced foot, circa 1745, 13cm. high. $320

GLASS

CANDLESTICKS

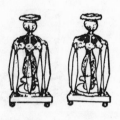

One of a pair of powder blue glass candlesticks, circa 1835, 17.5cm. high. $400

Pair of ormolu and crystal lustre sidepieces, circa 1830. $450

Unusual glass candlestick, 8¼in. high, with beaded high domed foot. $460

Airtwist glass candlestick with fluted cylindrical nozzle, circa 1750, 20cm. high. $500

Mid 19th century overlay lustre, one of a pair, 29.8cm. high. $520

Large cut glass column with faceted stem, circa 1900, 54.5cm. high. $520

Bronze and Favrile glass candlestick, by Tiffany, 8in. high. $605

Composite stemmed candlestick on radially ribbed domed foot, circa 1770, 26cm. high. $640

One of a pair of pressed glass candlesticks, Sandwich, Massachusetts, 1835-45, 7½in. high. $725

48

Rare glass candlestick, circa 1710, 7½in. high. $785

Pair of Regency period cut glass candlesticks with drops. $810

Pressed glass candlestick, Sandwich, Massachusetts, 1830-35, 6in. high. $825

Pressed glass candlestick in cobalt blue, Sandwich, Massachusetts, 1830-35, 5½in. high. $850

One of a pair of cut glass candlesticks, 9½in. high, circa 1800. $865

Rare blue nozzled candlestick, 7¼in. high, circa 1760. $925

Glass candlestick with a stem comprising different varieties of knops, 7¼ in. $1,590

One of a pair of Regency ormolu and cut-glass candlesticks, 39cm. high. $2,140

One of a pair of Tiffany bronze and glass candlesticks, 14½in. high. $4,500

GLASS

CAR MASCOTS

Frosted glass model of an eagle, 15.2cm. high. $80

Glass motor car mascot by Lalique, 9.7cm. high. $180

Lalique falcon's head car mascot. $250

Lalique 'Seagull in Flight' car mascot. $300

Lalique glass car mascot 'The Archer', molded in intaglio, 12.5cm. high. $585

Lalique 'St. Christopher' car mascot. $675

Lalique 'Vitesse' car mascot. $675

Lalique 'Spirit of the Wind' car mascot. $765

Lalique cock's head desk ornament, circa 1925, 20.25cm. high. $945

Lalique 'Dragonfly' mascot. $1,125

Lalique glass Longchamps mascot. $1,215

Lalique frosted glass mascot, circa 1920, 17.5cm. high. $1,240

Lalique glass hawk car mascot, 19cm. high, circa 1930. $1,575

'Spirit of the Wind' glass car mascot by Lalique, 19.5cm. long. $1,685

One of a pair of Lalique 'Dragonfly' car mascots mounted as bookends. $2,140

Lalique glass car mascot, 1920's, 14cm. wide. $2,475

Lalique glass figure of a cockerel, 1930's, 19.5cm. high. $2,970

Lalique glass car mascot, 'Spirit of the Wind', 1930's, 25.5cm. long. $4,050

GLASS

CARAFES

Late Victorian ruby glass carafe, 10in. high. $110

Ale carafe with cylindrical body and tapering neck, circa 1770, 25.5cm. high. $585

Diamond engraved magnum carafe of mallet shape, English, 1822. $1,100

CASKETS

Late 19th century ruby glass casket, 9cm. wide. $270

Palais Royal cut glass casket and cover with gilt metal mounts. $360

Blue glass casket with six perfume bottles, circa 1850, 15.2cm. wide. $475

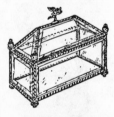

Bohemian ruby-stained casket with metal mounts, circa 1860, 16cm. wide. $545

'Bulle de Savon' opaline ormolu mounted casket with canted angles, circa 1830, 15cm. high. $820

Mid 17th century French rock crystal miniature casket, 4½in. long. $6,385

GLASS

CASTERS

Edwardian glass sugar caster with a plated lid. $25

Edwardian glass sugar caster with silver top. $35

CASTERS

Victorian ruby glass sugar sifter, with silver top. $45

CENTERPIECES

19th century cut glass and plated centerpiece. $105

One of a pair of Victorian plated bird stands with glass dishes. $245

Large silvered metal Art Nouveau centerpiece, with a glass bowl, circa 1900, 45cm. high. $720

Coffee and cream glass centerpiece by Webb, 10¼in. diameter. $780

Silver table centerpiece, Birmingham, 1866, 48oz., 21in. high. $900

George III centerpiece by Benjamin and James Smith, London 1810, 13½in. high, 103oz. 17dwt. $3,150

53

GLASS

CHAMPAGNE GLASSES

One of a set of six Edwardian champagne glasses. $60

Faceted champagne flute with plain round funnel bowl engraved round the rim, 1790, 17.1cm. high. $145

Pedestal stemmed champagne glass, rounded bowl with shallow pan-topped rim, circa 1745, 14.5cm. high. $155

Engraved ale or champagne flute, 1780, 19.7cm. high. $180

Pedestal stemmed champagne glass with double ogee bowl, circa 1745, 14.5cm. high. $195

Composite stemmed champagne glass with double ogee bowl, circa 1740, 15cm. high. $210

Composite stemmed champagne glass with double ogee bowl, circa 1740, 15cm. $210

Baluster champagne glass, circa 1720, 5½in. high. $395

Pedestal stemmed champagne glass with cup topped bowl on a hexagonal stem, circa 1745, 17cm. high. $835

54

A French lantern-shaped electric light, circa 1910, 97cm. $220

Art Nouveau brass and glass chandelier, circa 1900. $280

Art Deco wrought iron and Schneider glass chandelier, 1930's, 67cm. wide. $505

Opaque glass chandelier with eight slender twisted flowering stems, circa 1900, 28in. high. $565

A 19th century brass and glass chandelier with eight scrolled arms. $600

Early 19th century twelve light chandelier with cut glass drops. $660

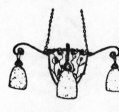

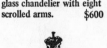

Daum glass and wrought iron chandelier, circa 1925, 62.5cm. wide. $675

A glass chandelier with eight fluted scroll branches. $720

Highly colored Belgian chandelier by Muller, 61cm. high. $750

GLASS

CHANDELIERS

A fine large early 19th century chandelier with crystal glass drops. $900

George III cut-glass chandelier 2ft. diam. $990

19th century crystal chandelier with ten scrolled ormolu arms, 3ft.6in. high. $1,235

Favrile glass and bronze chandelier by Tiffany Studios, 20in. high. $1,260

A large Edwardian salon chandelier with a fountain of glass drops, 107 cm. $1,800

Fine glass ceiling fixture by Rene Lalique, circa 1925, 10¾in. diam. $2,475

One of a pair of 19th century cut-glass chandeliers.$2,955

Iridescent Favrile glass chandelier by Tiffany, shade 14in. high. $3,035

Double overlay glass chandelier by Daum Freres, 15½in. diam.$3,150

Unusual leaded glass chandelier with pulley pull-down mechanism, 52½in. high. $3,575

Gilt bronze and Favrile glass ceiling fixture by Tiffany, 17in. high. $3,715

George III cut glass eight-light chandelier, 43in. high. $5,065

Late 19th century Venetian colored glass chandelier, 4ft.10in. high. $5,400

Rare green glass and bronze chandelier by Tiffany, 46in. high. $14,625

Favrile glass turtle-back and leaded glass chandelier by Tiffany, 34½in. high. $14,625

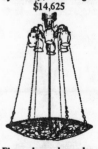

A superb 18th century English cut-glass chandelier. $15,600

Superb Adam style chandelier, circa 1785. $19,800

Fine and rare alamander leaded glass chandelier by Tiffany, 48in. high. $37,125

GLASS

CORDIAL GLASSES

George III cordial glass, with funnel bowl. $115

Opaque twist cordial glass, with funnel bowl, circa 1765, 14.5cm. high. $185

Cordial glass, ogee bowl set on a double series opaque-twist stem, circa 1760, 6¾in. high. $190

Cordial glass with small drawn trumpet bowl, circa 1745, 5¾in. high. $200

Opaque twist cordial glass with funnel bowl, circa 1770, 15.5cm. high. $205

Opaque twist cordial glass with funnel bowl, circa 1770, 15cm. high. $215

A Facon de Venise cordial glass, 17th century, 4¼in. high. $260

Cordial wine glass with small straight sided bowl, 1770, 13.9cm. high.$270

Cordial glass with a flared bucket bowl, 6¾in. high, circa 1760. $290

58

GLASS

CORDIAL GLASSES

Engraved cordial glass with trumpet bowl set on plain drawn stem and conical foot, 1745, 17.8cm. high. **$290**

Air twist cordial glass with fine drawn trumpet bowl set on a multi-ply mercury air twist stem, 1745, 14cm. high. **$290**

Engraved cordial glass with small bowl molded to half height, 1770, 17.1cm. high. **$325**

Cordial glass with bowl engraved with flowers and leaves, 1780, 16.5cm. high. **$325**

Cordial glass with small ogee bowl, circa 1760, 7½in. high. **$335**

Engraved cordial glass with small bowl molded to half height, 1770, 17.1cm. high. **$340**

Cordial glass with cylindrical bowl, circa 1730, 6½in. high. **$340**

Plain stemmed cordial glass with pan-topped bucket bowl, circa 1745, 16.5cm. high. **$425**

Cordial glass with small ogee bowl, 6¾in. high, circa 1760. **$450**

59

CORDIAL GLASSES

Engraved plain stemmed cordial glass of drawn trumpet shape, Irish, circa 1745, 18cm. high. $475

Irish engraved cordial glass with funnel bowl, probably Dublin, circa 1740, 16.5cm. high. $525

Opaque twist cordial glass with funnel bowl, circa 1765, 17cm. high. $690

Baluster cordial glass with bell bowl, circa 1720, 16.5cm. high. $715

Engraved air twist cordial glass of drawn trumpet shape, circa 1750, 17cm. high. $730

Rare pink twist cordial glass, circa 1760, 5½in. high. $900

Baluster cordial glass with flared bowl, circa 1720, 7in. high. $905

Rare Beilby color twist cordial glass engraved with leaves, circa 1770, 17.5cm. high. $4,800

Rare Beilby color twist cordial glass with small funnel bowl, circa 1770, 17.5cm. high. $7,200

Late 19th century four-bottle plated cruet. $90

Victorian plated cruet stand complete with six cut-glass bottles. $90

A small four bottle plated cruet. $125

Victorian six bottle plated cruet with cut glass bottles. $125

Small silver novelty cruet in the form of a roller skate which carries the mark for 1837. $125

A fine Victorian seven bottle cruet with cut glass bottles. $145

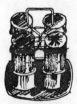

Four bottle silver cruet, by R. Cattle and J. Barber, York, circa 1810. $185

American amberina castor set, circa 1890, in plated silver frame. $350

Seven bottle silver condiment set, dated 1868. $435

CRUETS

William IV silver cruet with cut-glass bottles. $440

George IV silver boat-shaped cruet set and stand by H. M. London, circa 1822-23. $485

18th century six bottle Dublin cruet by G. Hill, 1766. $810

Georgian five bottle pierced silver cruet by T. Dealtry, London, 1776. $825

Rare set of enameled 'mock china' cruet bottles, circa 1760, 4¾in. to 7¼in. $2,250

A good George III Warwick cruet. $2,265

Table cruet by Paul Storr, London, 1811, 30oz. $3,040

A pair of Louis XVI two-bottle cruets, 12¾in. wide, by Jacques Favre, Paris, 1778, 51oz.1dwt. $3,825

Early George II two-bottle cruet frame by Paul de Lamerie, London, 1728, 5½in. wide, 14oz.13dwt. $11,250

Early 20th century green and clear glass cup with silver rim. $18

Victorian cranberry glass custard cup. $22

Custard glass with strongly ribbed funnel bowl with everted rim, circa 1750, 4½in. high. $115

One of a pair of Chinese cherry red wine cups, 18th century, 3in. high. $180

New England peach blown punch cup with ribbed handle, 2¼in. high. $180

One of a pair of unusual punch or custard cups, circa 1790, 8cm. high. $270

Early engraved custard glass, 5in. high, circa 1730. $270

Double handled posset cup, 3¾in. high, circa 1720. $325

A custard glass with round funnel bowl, 18th century, 4¼in. high. $475

CUPS

Rare early posset cup, 3½in. high, circa 1690.$565

Agata peachblow punch cup by the New England Glass Co., circa 1887, 2½in. high. $600

Early 19th century Swiss gold and enamel zarf, 2¼in. high. $620

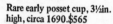

Tiffany gold iridescent loving cup with three handles, 5in. high. $820

Turquoise opaline ormolu mounted cabinet cup and saucer, circa 1830, cup with double scroll handle. $820

Galle cameo glass stemmed honeycomb cup, 11.75cm. high, circa 1900. $1,465

Late 19th century Viennese enamel and rock crystal cup by Hermann Ratzersdorfer, 22.5cm. high. $7,020

Late 19th century Viennese enamel and rock crystal peacock cup, 25.7cm. high, by Hermann Ratzersdorfer. $7,720

Mold blown glass cup of the 1st century A.D., 2½in. high. $168,750

GLASS

DECANTERS

Victorian etched glass decanter. $18

Cut glass wine decanter and stopper, etched with vines. $30

19th century cut glass decanter. $35

Late Victorian bulbous cut glass decanter, 8½ in. high. $40

Art Deco mallet-shaped decanter. $55

Victorian hand-painted decanter. $55

A stirrup glass decanter, circa 1820. $55

19th century cut crystal decanter of shouldered shape, 33 cm. high. $60

Early 19th century plain glass decanter. $60

GLASS

DECANTERS

Early 19th century barrel-shaped decanter. $90

One of a pair of Victorian pear-shaped decanters, 22.5cm. high. $90

A cut crystal glass decanter, circa 1890, 9¾in. high. $100

A green Bristol decanter. $100

Late 18th century plain club-shaped decanter. $120

Georgian engraved decanter, circa 1780. $125

Blue overlay decanter, circa 1845. $130

Bristol blue glass decanter, circa 1800. $140

A Bristol amethyst decanter with a silver cork stopper. $140

Mid 19th century green Mary Gregory decanter depicting a boy in white. $150

A pair of 18th century green glass spirit bottles, 11½in. high. $150

Rounded base decanter engraved with floral festoons, with a snake coiled round the neck, circa 1840. $160

Late 18th century engraved decanter. $160

19th century glass decanter, Bristol red, with plated stopper. $165

One of a pair of late 19th century cut crystal spirit decanters, 9½in. high. $170

Rock crystal engraved decanter, probably by J. Keller, 10½ in. high, circa 1885. $175

Blown Masonic clear glass decanter with fluted bottom border, 28cm. high. $175

Early 19th century ship's decanter. $180

DECANTERS

Quart-sized decanter with a central bank of diamond shaped cutting, circa 1810. $180

18th century decanter engraved 'Burgundy'. $180

Large glass decanter, 11in. high, circa 1830, marked R.B. Cooper's Patent. $215

Bottle decanter and stopper, globular body molded with 'nipt diamond waies', circa 1740, 26cm. high. $230

Engraved clear glass and blue overlay decanter and stopper, circa 1929, 28.2cm. high. $250

Heavy ship's decanter, circa 1860. $270

One of a pair of cut glass decanters and stoppers, circa 1810, 10½in. high. $280

Adam style cut and engraved lipped and shouldered decanter, circa 1770. $305

Engraved bottle decanter and stopper, 1731, with globular body inscribed with the initials RL, 26cm. high. $310

Engraved decanter and stopper of Jacobite significance, decorated with flowers, circa 1760, 27cm. high. $310

Engraved decanter and stopper of club shape, for 'Whiteport', circa 1760, 24cm. high. $310

Lalique glass decanter of flattened oval section, 27cm. high, 1930's. $340

One of a pair of English decanters and stoppers, circa 1820, 9¼in. high. $340

Sunderland Bridge engraved decanter, circa 1840. $345

One of four glass Horn of Plenty decanters, American, circa 1850. $350

Quart-sized, wheel engraved decanter with thistles and roses and triple plain ringed neck, circa 1790. $360

Barrel-shaped decanter by the Waterloo Glass Co., Cork, circa 1820, 27cm. high. $370

Norwegian decanter of spherical form, 8¼in. high, circa 1835. $385

DECANTERS

Lynn bottle-decanter, globular body with horizontal ribbing, circa 1770, 18.5cm. high. $385

Engraved decanter and stopper of mallet shape, circa 1765, 29cm. high. $425

Engraved decanter and stopper of mallet shape, 'Madeira' in a floral cartouche, circa 1760, 29.5cm. high. $425

One of a pair of decanters with broad bands of flute and diamond cutting, circa 1810. $430

Bohemian or Spanish enameled milchglas decanter and stopper, circa 1780, 11¼in. high. $445

One of a pair of engraved decanters, circa 1760, 9½in. high. $450

Blown three-mold miniature decanter, Sandwich, Massachusetts, circa 1828, 3½in. high. $450

Pair of Victorian glass gilded decanters, circa 1860, 12in. high. $450

Sunderland Bridge decanter and stopper, circa 1820, 9½in. high. $450

Large green glass decanter and spire stopper, circa 1850, 52cm. high. $470

20th century enameled decanter of Persian interest, 26.8cm. high. $495

One of a pair of English decanters, circa 1820, 9¾in. high. $495

One of a pair of Irish cut glass decanters and stoppers, circa 1810. $520

One of a pair of engraved glass decanters, circa 1780, 25cm. high. $525

One of a pair of late 18th century Venetian glass decanters and stoppers. $540

St. Louis decanter, 21.5cm. high, with dark blue and opaque white bands. $540

One of a pair of blue glass decanters, 10in. high, circa 1800. $540

One of a pair of Cork Glass Co. engraved decanters with bull's eye stoppers, circa 1800. $540

GLASS

DECANTERS

Ship's decanter with flute cutting and double ringed neck, circa 1810. $540

Engraved decanter and stopper of mallet shape, with Cyder inscription, circa 1765, 28cm. high. $545

Engraved glass decanter and stopper, circa 1800, 20.5cm. high. $545

Williamite decanter and stopper, 9½in. high, circa 1800. $565

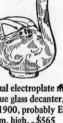

Unusual electroplate mounted blue glass decanter, circa 1900, probably English, 29.8cm. high. $565

One of three English blue tinted decanters, early 19th century, 11¼in. high. $615

Dutch 19th century decanter with silver mounts. $630

18th century marriage decanter with cut spire stopper. $660

Silesian cut decanter bottle and stopper, circa 1730, 11¾in. high. $675

72

Rare bottle-decanter with square body, circa 1730, 35cm. high. $685

Early 19th century Cork engraved decanter, 10½in. high. $700

Shouldered mallet shaped decanter, engraved 'Port', circa 1770. $720

Irish cut glass magnum armorial decanter and stopper, circa 1810. $720

One of a pair of Baccarat decanters with silver gilt caps, Paris 1819-38. $720

One of a set of four decanters with bands of diamond flute and step cutting, circa 1810. $720

A glass decanter by Rene Lalique, 12ins. high. $720

Good Bohemian green decanter and stopper, circa 1850, 48cm. high, with triple ringed neck. $740

Enamelled decanter jug and stopper with flattened body, circa 1870, 31.5cm. high. $790

GLASS

DECANTERS

Unusual facet cut blue glass decanter, 10½in. high, circa 1760. $870

Glass serving-bottle with square body and slender tapering neck, circa 1740, 18cm. high. $865

WMF pewter mounted green glass decanter, circa 1900, 38.5cm. high. $890

One of a pair of green glass decanters, 9in. high, circa 1800. $810

One of a pair of ship's decanters with flute cutting and bull's eye stoppers, circa 1810. $900

One of a pair of Sunderland Bridge decanters and stoppers, circa 1820, 9½in. high. $1,045

One of a pair of William IV mahogany holders and glass decanters, 1ft.4in. high, 7in. diam. $1,080

Two of a set of three green tinted spirit decanters, 8in. high, circa 1800. $1,285

Jacobite decanter, circa 1760, 10in. high. $1,240

Green glass decanter by J. Giles, 9¼in. high, circa 1775. $1,295

One of a pair of rare Apsley Pellatt encrusted decanters, 10in. high, circa 1820. $1,500

Signed and dated decanter and stopper by L. Whistler, 1973, 28.8cm. high. $1,530

One of a pair of engraved decanters, 11½in. high, circa 1750, with tapering necks. $1,530

Large Bohemian enameled decanter and stopper, circa 1850, 54cm. high. $1,780

Late 19th century Persian glass decanter with portraits. $1,980

Large glass decanter and stopper, circa 1850, 56cm. high. $2,115

Very rare Giles opaque white decanter, 11½in. high, circa 1775. $2,140

An English glass decanter, 10½in. high. $2,445

DECANTERS

Early globe and shaft wine bottle, circa 1660, 9in. high. $3,040

A Bristol opaque white decanter and stopper. $3,170

A Ravenscroft decanter jug, circa 1685. $4,500

A fine English decanter and stopper of blue glass with gilding, 27.3 cm. $4,500

Silver mounted green glass decanter by the Guild of Handicrafts Ltd., 1901, 20.5 cm. $4,950

Late 17th century English decanter jug complete with stopper. $5,035

George III Waterford glass decanter, 20in. high, circa 1780. $5,625

One of a pair of George III Waterford glass decanters, 19in. high, circa 1780. $7,270

Glass decanter jug by G. Ravenscroft with a heart-shaped lid. $11,250

Small early 19th century mahogany decanter box containing four decanters. $160

A George III satinwood and kingwood banded decanter box, the lid and front inlaid with shields, 7 in. wide. $305

Georgian mahogany decanter set with six Venetian gilt decorated spirit decanters, circa 1795. $345

Coromandel and brass mounted liquor casket fitted with four cut glass decanters. $395

Mahogany and inlaid decanter box with four cut glass decanters, 8½in. high. $425

Set of six decanters, circa 1795. $435

19th century rosewood travelling drinks cabinet. $475

'Directore' mahogany decanter box, 19½in. high, circa 1912. $675

Walnut decanter box in well-figured and burr-wood, 28cm. wide, circa 1870. $695

GLASS

DECANTER BOXES

Early 19th century mahogany and brass bound decanter case, 22cm. wide.
$730

George III mahogany decanter box, fully fitted.
$990

Mid 19th century English kingwood and mother-of-pearl bombe liqueur cabinet, 11 x 13½in. $1,020

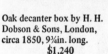

Mid 19th century scarlet boulle tantalus with fitted interior, 13½in. wide.
$1,125

Oak decanter box by H. H. Dobson & Sons, London, circa 1850, 9¾in. long.
$1,240

An ebony decanter suite contained in a case inlaid with the Imperial Eagle and Bees. $1,275

Superb cased set of nine late 17th century cordial or spirit clear glass bottles in a wrought iron banded oak case, circa 1690.
$1,350

Early 18th century Austro-Hungarian octagonal casket containing twelve gilt decorated glass bottles, 26.5cm wide. $1,500

Travelling decanter case with glasses and decanters.
$1,915

GLASS

Victorian decanter stand with cut glass bottles. $110

A Victorian silver plated tantalus of three cut-glass decanters. $220

Silver plated decanter stand holding three colored glass bottles. $235

Silver plated wine cruet of trefoil shape, 16½in. high, fitted with three bottles. $310

English electroplated tri-form decanter stand, 48cm. high, circa 1860, with three blue glass bottles. $495

Electroplated three-bottle frame and three wine labels, circa 1850, 45.3cm. high. $610

Set of three blue glass decanters and stand, 19th century, 9½in. high. $615

Set of four green tinted gilt decanters, stoppers and stand, circa 1790, 9¾in. high. $780

Rectangular two-bottle decanter stand by Reily & Storer, London, 1836, 26cm. long, 28.6oz. $980

DISHES

Small Victorian ruby
glass dish with wavy
edge, 4in. diam.
$25

Victorian cranberry glass
jam dish in a plated
stand. $65

Victorian ruby glass double
bon bon dish in a plated
stand. $100

A Lalique glass circular
dish, with groups of
birds in relief, 8½ins.
diam. $145

Late 19th century Eastern
United States cut-glass dish
in cornucopia and cross-
hatch patterns. $225

Late 19th century gilt and
enameled glass dish.$250

Mary Gregory enameled
dish with everted rim,
circa 1880, 13½in. diam.
          $300

Green glass dish of shallow
rounded form, 1st century
A.D., 7½in. diam.
          $340

Smoked glass dish with
everted rim molded with
three sea nymphs, 1930's,
marked 'A. Verlys, France',
38.75cm. diam. $375

Lalique opalescent glass dish and cover, 1920's, 17cm. diam. $400

Late 19th/early 20th century gilt metal mounted rock crystal pedestal dish, 11cm. high. $610

Daum etched and enameled glass dish with two loop handles, 18.5cm. wide, circa 1900. $675

Small colorless glass dish with rounded sides and twin handles, 2nd-3rd century A.D., 4¼in. wide. $675

A high quality pate de cristal dish by Argy Rosseau. $685

Galle glass dish carved as a shell, 1890's, 34cm. long. $745

Daum cameo glass dish, 14.5cm. wide, circa 1900. $900

Daum cameo glass dish and cover, circa 1900, 9.5cm. $945

Rare Silesian Schwarzlot armorial dish, circa 1745, 8¼in. diam. $955

GLASS

DISHES

Antique silveria dish by Royal Brierley Crystal, 1901. $955

Boat-shaped dish signed R. Lalique, France, in frosted glass with pierced handles, 52cm. long. $1,170

Daum cameo glass dish and cover, circa 1900, 8.7cm. wide. $1,200

Small late 19th century Viennese enamel and rock crystal covered vase and circular dish by Hermann Ratzersdorfer. $1,405

Webb cameo shallow circular dish, 8½in. diam. $1,745

Venetian Latticinio (vetra di trina) large circular dish, circa 1700, 49.5cm. diam. $1,800

Early 20th century fluted oval rock crystal dish, probably Austrian, 16.2cm. long. $1,870

Viennese enamel and rock crystal dish with hardstone medallion, late 19th century, 17cm. diam. $1,870

Mid 16th century Venetian gilt and enameled dish, 5¾in. diam. $3,040

SWEETMEAT

DISHES

Sweetmeat dish, shallow double ogee bowl with a band of Lozenge cutting, circa 1770, 15.5cm. high. $50

Cut-glass sweetmeat dish, the double ogee bowl with a band of oval within lozenge cutting, circa 1770, 15cm. high. $85

Double-ogeed sweet-meat dish, 6½in. high, circa 1730. $95

Cut glass sweetmeat glass, with double ogee bowl, 6in. high. $115

Balustroid sweetmeat glass, 3¾in. high. $125

Sweetmeat dish on star-studded pedestal stem, 6in. high, circa 1730. $180

Silesian stemmed sweetmeat glass, 6¼in. high. $180

Late 17th century sweet-meat glass with gadrooned bowl, 9cm. high. $190

Sweetmeat dish with ribbed double ogee bowl, circa 1730, 6¼in. high. $200

DISHES
SWEETMEAT

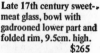

Pedestal stemmed sweet-meat glass with double ogee bowl and domed and ribbed foot, circa 1745, 14.5cm. high.
$215

18th century glass sweet-meat dish on tripod scroll feet, 6.5cm. high.
$250

Late 17th century sweet-meat glass, bowl with gadrooned lower part and folded rim, 9.5cm. high.
$265

Sweetmeat dish with double ogee bowl, 6¼in. high, circa 1730. $270

Early sweetmeat dish, with shallow bowl and gadrooned base, 3¼in. high, circa 1720.
$270

Rare sweetmeat glass with flared ribbed bowl, circa 1730, 7in. high. $285

Sweetmeat glass with double ogee bowl, on domed and folded foot, circa 1740, 8cm. high.
$290

Late 17th century sweet-meat dish, 3½in. with bucket-shaped bowl. $330

Sweetmeat dish with three base collars, 6¼in. high, circa 1730. $345

Fine Anglo-Venetian sweetmeat dish, circa 1700, 3¼in.
high. $350

'Opale' opaline ormolu
mounted oval sweetmeat
dish with marble striations
in the glass, circa 1830,
15cm. wide. $505

Unusual sweetmeat dish,
with double ogee bowl,
7in. high, circa 1760.
                       $520

Unusual sweetmeat bowl,
5½in. high, circa 1740.
                    $540

Unusual sweetmeat dish,
with cup-shaped bowl,
3¾in. high, circa 1720.
                    $620

Bobbin-knopped sweetmeat
dish, with double ogee
bowl, 5¼in. high, circa
1740. $620

Early 18th century
English sweetmeat
dish. $675

Early English sweetmeat
dish. $735

Small baluster sweetmeat
glass with double ogee
bowl, circa 1725, 10cm.
high. $865

GLASS

DRINKING GLASSES

Tot glass with stylised engraving. $5

Bohemian ruby and engraved grapevine drinking glass. $25

Engraved ruby sherry glass, circa 1825. $30

Gin glass with thick ribbed bowl, circa 1780. $55

A Mary Gregory glass depicting a girl. $55

Dram glass with a round bowl engraved with a fruiting vine and bird, circa 1750. $60

Dram or spirit glass with molded cup bowl on a plain stem, 1780, 9.9cm high. $90

Coaching glass with faceted ball knop joined to an ogee bowl by a collar, 1820, 12.6cm. high. $110

18th century dram glass with ogee bowl, 4¼in. high. $155

GLASS

Biedermeier drinking glass in Bristol blue and pink with etched banded panel, 6in. high. $170

Hexagonal Biedermeier drinking glass in ruby red with oval gilt banded green panels, 5in. high. $180

17th/18th century boot glass, possibly Liege, 15cm. high. $910

Rare opaque twist engraved cider glass, inscribed 'Cyder', circa 1765, 20.4cm. high. $1,745

17th century Daumenglas and cover, 9¾in. high. $1,755

German puzzle glass, 11in. high. $2,350

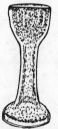

Large internally decorated glass chalice by Maurice Marinot, late 1920's, 33.5cm. high. $6,300

German passglas, 1725, 24cm. high. $7,290

17th/18th century Franconian drinking glass, 15cm. high, with enameled decoration. $12,375

87

EPERGNES

Victorian spatter glass epergne. $55

Victorian cut glass centerpiece $100

Victorian cranberry glass four branch epergne. $100

Victorian white opaque glass flower and fruit epergne. $110

Unusual Victorian cranberry glass epergne with plated mounts, 11¾in. high. $135

Victorian vaseline glass vase with opaque frilly edges on top and bottom rims, circa 1860, 6in. high. $135

Victorian satin glass fruit and flower epergne. $140

Late 19th century Eastern United States three-branch cranberry glass epergne, 20½in. high. $175

Victorian opaque glass epergne. $180

Victorian three-branch opaline glass epergne. $190

Victorian crimson glass epergne with center trumpet, 60cm. high overall. $225

Fine quality 19th century plated epergne. $440

Silver plated epergne, circa 1825, 15½in. high. $790

A Victorian silver gilt epergne by Hunt & Roskell. $1,370

Silver epergne supporting engraved glass vase and dishes, by Elkington & Co., Birmingham, 1907, 1,457gm. of silver. $1,395

George III silver gilt epergne with glass dishes by M. T., London, 1806. $1,405

A parcel gilt epergne by Elkington & Co., 1875, 141 oz. $3,420

George III four-branch epergne by Matthew Boulton, Birmingham, 1811, 8½in. high, 64oz.2dwt. $3,600

EWERS

Victorian cut glass ewer with fern decoration. $45

A blue glass ewer ornament decorated by Mary Gregory, 43cm. high. $115

Victorian frosted and cut glass ewer, 14in. high. $170

An early English glass ewer engraved with hops and barley, circa 1760. $210

Central European gilt milch-glas ewer, 5½in. high, circa 1740. $450

French Empire style silver and cut crystal ewer, 25cm. high. $450

Large cut glass ewer in neo-classical style, English, circa 1830, 10½in. high. $500

Late 19th century glass ewer mounted in silver-gilt, 16 in. high. $615

Frosted glass wine ewer by C. and G. Fox 1856, with silver gilt mounts. $720

Rainbow satin glass ewer in herringbone pattern with mother-of-pearl finish, 10in. high. $970

Early 18th century baluster-shaped glass jug with loop handle, 14cm. high. $1,000

A rare 17th century diamond-point engraved ewer. $1,370

One of a pair of French champagne jugs with silver colored metal mounts, circa 1900, 27.4cm. high. $2,340

16th or early 17th century Facon de Venise Latticinio ewer, South Netherlands or Venetian, 16.5cm. high. $2,475

Catalan Latticinio ewer of the 17th/18th century, 7in. high. $2,550

A Victorian red glass wine ewer. $2,880

Late 16th century Venetian amethyst baluster ewer, 9½in. high. $4,950

William IV frosted glass ewer with silver gilt mounts by Paul Storr, London, 1836, 8¾in. high. $7,875

GLASS

FIGURES

Pate de verre study of a stag beetle by Almeric Walter. $375

Walter pate de verre figure of a peahen, 19cm. long, 1920's. $1,015

Large Lalique frosted glass figure of a pigeon, 14.5cm. high, 1930's. $1,125

Galle faience cat, enameled mark E. Galle Nancy, 1880's, 34cm. high. $1,125

Rare 18th century Venetian figurine, 6in. high, in opaque white glass. $1,350

Lalique smoked glass figure of 'Suzanne au Bain', 22.75cm. high, 1920's. $1,390

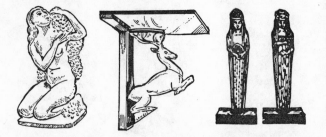

20th century Lalique glass figure of a kneeling woman, 21cm. high. $2,250

Lalique glass bracket shelf, 1930's, 26.25cm. wide. $3,040

Pair of figures by Lalique in frosted glass, 56cm. high. $6,750

FLASKS

Late Victorian pressed glass scent flask. $15

Victorian cranberry glass flask. $50

Translucent Roman green glass flask. $60

Cut glass flask, possibly Waterford, circa 1800, 19cm. long. $80

Nailsea flask in the form of a pair of bellows. $125

19th century Nailsea flask. $135

Unusual engraved glass pilgrim flask with flattened ovoid body, circa 1860, 29cm. high, set on wood base. $340

Colorless glass flask with spherical body, circa 3rd century A.D., 4¾in. high. $340

Milchglas Central-European flask with pewter mount, 5in. high, circa 1750.$360

94

GLASS

Plain firing glass with trumpet bowl set on thick flat foot, 1740, 8.8cm. high. $125

Opaque twist firing glass set on double series twist stem, 1770, 10cm. high. $145

Masonic firing glass of trumpet shape, 3¾in. h $160

Opaque twist firing glass set on double series twist stem, 1770, 10cm. high. $225

A pair of Jacobite firing glasses, 3½in. high, circa 1750. $490

Scottish Jacobite opaque twist firing glass, 3½in. high. $620

Enameled masonic firing glass, 4in. high, circa 1750. $735

Color twist firing glass with small ovoid bowl, circa 1760, 4in. high. $2,475

Jacobite portrait firin 3½in. high, circa 175 $2,925

One of a pair of enameled moon flasks, circa 1870, 21cm. high. $375

Central European enameled flask, 6½in. high, circa 1750. $460

Central European milchglas flask, circa 1750, 5in. high. $465

Central European enameled flask, circa 1750, 5in. high. $490

Bohemian Lithyalin flask and stopper of marbled glass, circa 1840, 33cm. high. $525

Central European enameled flask, circa 1750, 21.5cm. ligh. $540

Unusual enameled flask in turquoise glass, circa 1875, 13.8cm. high. $540

Manganese purple glass flask of cylindrical form, 3rd-4th century A.D., 4¼in. high. $540

Early flattened oviform flask, circa 1690, 5½in. high. $595

GLASS

FLASKS

Colorless glass flask with dome-shaped body, 4th-5th century A.D., 4¾in. high. $630

Early 18th century miniature European enameled flask, 3in. high. $750

Thüringian engraved flask, circa 1690, 10½in. high. $755

Small pale yellowish Islamic glass pilgrim flask, circa 13th century, 3¼in. high. $765

German glass enameled flask, circa 1728, 8¼in. high. $810

Central European flask with enameled decoration, circa 1740, 17.5cm. high. $855

Central European enameled glass flask with pewter screw cap, circa 1750, 21cm. high. $950

Galle purple flask with everted rim, circa 1900, 13cm. high. $1,125

German enameled dated hunting flask, 1802, 5½in. high. $1,125

Rare coldpainted Venetian ring flask, 11¼in. high, 16th century.
$1,240

Central European enameled flask, 18cm. high, circa 1750. $1,295

Early 18th century bottle-shaped flask of dark blue, 7½in. high, Netherlandish.
$1,465

Bohemian or Franconian tailor's enameled blue cylindrical flask, dated 1673, 14.5cm. high.
$1,690

Late 17th century South German ruby glass baluster flask with applied rim foot, 15cm. high. $2,510

Venetian 'Calcedonio' flask of shouldered hexagonal form, 17th century. $2,590

Mid 18th century Bohemian chinoiserie scent flask. $3,000

Bohemian enameled glass flask, circa 1661.
$12,375

One of a pair of rare Hausmaler flasks by Ignaz Preissler. $30,000

97

FLUTE GLASSES

An unusual amethyst glass, circa 1850. $110

Multiple series air twist wine glass, circa 1760. $125

Drawn trumpet bowl glass with double series opaque twist stem, circa 1760. $145

Early English water flute wine glass, 6¼ins. high. $160

Early English flute glass. $325

Mixed-twist wine flute of trumpet shape, circa 1760, 19cm. high. $410

Ale flute with slender trumpet bowl, circa 1750, $525

Balustroid ale-flute with slender bell bowl, 1730, 18.5cm. high. $1,310

Flute glass with the Arms of Charles II and James II engraved in diamond point, made of soda glass and almost certainly Dutch, 15½ins. high. $7,590

Large ruby tinted goblet with gilt flecking and Griffon pattern stem, 37.5cm. high. $45

Large ruby tinted and gilt decorated goblet with applied moldings , on knopped stem, 26cm. high. $70

Conical bowled goblet engraved with a continuous stag, circa 1730 8 in. high. $80

Victorian red and white Bohemian glass goblet. $90

Mammoth cut-glass goblet with large bucket bowl, circa 1840, 35.2cm. high. $125

One of a pair of red glass Bohemian goblets and covers, circa 1814, 16½in. high. $130

Crystal glass goblet, circa 1800. $145

Air twist goblet , ogee bowl with honey-comb molded lower part, circa 1750, 17cm. high. $155

Composite stemmed goblet with flared straight-sided bowl, circa 1750, 19.5cm. high. $170

GOBLETS

Sunderland Bridge goblet. $175

Biedermeier green glass goblet, finely etched with deer, 6¼in. high. $180

Amber flashed goblet, circa 1850, 14.5cm. high. $200

German engraved goblet on square base, 5in. high, circa 1815. $235

Pedestal stemmed glass goblet with hexagonally molded stem on folded foot, circa 1730, 16.5cm. high. $265

Victorian Bohemian 'documentary' stained glass goblet, engraved on one side, with faceted stem and circular foot, 1851. $280

Engraved goblet with ovoid bowl, 9in. high, circa 1745. $290

Green goblet of bright emerald color, plain stem on spirally-molded foot, circa 1760, 13.5cm. high. $295

Tall engraved goblet, 47.5cm. high, circa 1880, with funnel bowl. $305

Baluster wine goblet with funnel bowl, 5¾in. high, circa 1700. $310

One of a set of four engraved goblets, circa 1870, 18.5cm. high. $310

Bohemian engraved goblet with funnel bowl, circa 1720, 9½in. high. $325

Goblet of dark emerald green tint, circa 1760, 13.5cm. high. $335

Portrait overlay goblet with round funnel bowl, circa 1850, 14.5cm. high. $350

Mixed twist wine goblet with very large bowl, 1760, 19.1cm. $360

Opaque twist goblet, ogee bowl with honey-comb molded lower part, circa 1765, 19cm. high. $380

Dutch engraved friendship goblet with slightly waisted bowl inscribed 'De Goede Vrindschap', circa 1765, 28cm. high. $390

Good ruby stained goblet and cover, circa 1850, 32cm. high. $395

GOBLETS

An early goblet with raspberry prunts and a silver mount to the foot dated 1924, $395

Large fox-hunting goblet, 7¼in. high, circa 1760. $405

Baluster wine goblet with round funnel bowl, circa 1710, 6½in. high. $420

Bohemian pink stained goblet and cover, circa 1850, 31cm. high. $420

Lauenstein goblet with waisted bowl, circa 1745, engraved with scenes of the seasons, 23cm. high. $430

Green goblet with oviform knopped stem with vertical flutes, late 18th century, 16.5cm. high. $435

One of a pair of 1851 Great Exhibition goblets, both wheel engraved with scenes of Windsor Castle, 5¼ in. high. $460

Dutch engraved goblet, circa 1740, 21.5cm. high, with thistle bowl. $475

Heavy baluster glass goblet with flared funnel bowl, circa 1705, 18cm. high. $480

GLASS

Pedestal stemmed glass goblet with flared trumpet bowl, circa 1745, 18cm. high. $480

Unusual green tinted wine goblet, 6¾in. high, circa 1730. $485

Lauenstein cut, gilt armorial goblet of 'sick' metal, circa 1730, 8¼in. high. $485

Bohemian engraved goblet, set on wrythen knop, circa 1730, 17.5cm. high. $495

Rare Bohemian engraved goblet, circa 1810, 11cm. high. $500

Unusual Sunderland Bridge goblet, 6¾in. high, 1859. $500

One of a set of four finely engraved goblets, circa 1870, 16.4cm. high. $500

Baluster goblet with tulip-shaped bowl having solid lower part, circa 1725, 17cm. high. $525

Giant engraved goblet, circa 1800, 11½in. high. $560

103

GOBLETS

Pedestal stemmed goblet with panel molded waisted ogee bowl, circa 1745, 19cm. high. $570

19th century Bohemian amber overlay glass goblet and cover, 17½in. high. $575

Large engraved goblet, 9½in. high, circa 1700, with replaced foot. $580

Dutch armorial goblet, funnel bowl engraved with the arms of the Province of Transylvania, circa 1765, 20.5cm. high. $585

A goblet with a large straight sided bowl, honeycombe molded 9¼ in., circa 1760. $600

Large gilded goblet with ogee bowl on plain columnar stem and conical foot, 1750, 18.3cm. $600

Jacobite goblet with bucket bowl decorated with rose and single bud, circa 1750, 8½in. high. $620

Bohemian pink-flash goblet and cover engraved in the manner of Pfohl, circa 1870, 32cm. high. $625

Baluster goblet with slender bell bowl supported on an annulated knop, circa 1715, 21cm. high. $665

Heavy baluster goblet with funnel bowl supported on a cyst above a ball knop, circa 1700, 17cm. high. $665

Bohemian engraved goblet and cover, circa 1700, 13½in. high. $685

Dutch engraved goblet with funnel bowl, circa 1765, 23cm., sold with cover. $720

Large baluster goblet, 8¾in. high, circa 1710. $725

Jacobite balustroid goblet with thistle-shaped bowl, circa 1740, 17cm. high. $765

Saxon engraved goblet with thistle bowl, 21cm. high, circa 1740. $781

Dutch engraved Newcastle goblet with putto and cartouches, circa 1745, 18cm. high. $810

Bohemian engraved color twist goblet and cover, circa 1760, 24cm. high. $840

Dutch engraved goblet with waisted bowl, circa 1745, 18.8cm. high. $855

GLASS

GOBLETS

Balustroid coin goblet with bell bowl, 7in. high. $865

Massive Bohemian blue overlay goblet engraved with a hunting scene, circa 1860, 37cm. high. $865

Rare electioneering goblet, the bowl inscribed 'Success to Sir Francis Knollys', circa 1745, 19cm. high. $900

Netherlandish engraved goblet with flared funnel bowl, circa 1700, 16cm. high. $900

Rare two-handled coin goblet, circa 1710, 6in. high. $945

A large lead glass goblet with prunts on the stem, 12½ins., circa 1790. $980

Saxon friendship goblet engraved with conjoined hearts and an inscription, circa 1730, 19.3cm. high. $990

Russian engraved goblet with the cypher of Empress Elizabeth Petrovna, circa 1740, 24cm. high. $1,015

Massive Jacobite air-twist goblet with funnel bowl, circa 1785, 17.5cm. high. $1,015

106

Silesian engraved goblet with fluted oval quatre-foil ogee bowl, circa 1750, 17.5cm. high. $1,015

Bohemian round funnel bowled goblet engraved with figures of a Boar Hunt circa 1740. $1,050

Early glass-of-lead goblet of Ravenscroft period, circa 1675, 11½in. high. $1,080

Large baluster goblet with funnel bowl, circa 1710, 23.5cm. high. $1,240

Unusual blue baluster goblet with funnel bowl, early 18th century, 16cm. $1,265

Victorian overlay goblet 1850, cup-shaped bowl with crenallated rim, on a single knop and tall foot. $1,320

Engraved Bohemian goblet, 7¼in. high, circa 1730. $1,350

Potsdam goblet and cover engraved with Russian emblems, 11½in. high, circa 1730. $1,350

Dutch engraved goblet of Newcastle type, circa 1750, 8½in. high. $1,410

GLASS

GOBLETS

Large Dutch engraved armorial goblet, 9¾in. high, circa 1780. $1,430

Elegant German goblet, about 1780, decorated with colored enamel. $1,450

Venetian or Anglo-Netherlandish Facon de Venise goblet, circa 1670, 25cm. high. $1,465

Mammoth engraved baluster goblet, circa 1710. $1,475

Engraved Potsdam goblet and cover, 12¼in. high, circa 1730. $1,520

A Dutch engraved Royal Armorial goblet with the Royal Arms of England, 20.5 cm. high. $1,530

Very large glass goblet, circa 1700, bowl with gadrooned lower part, 22cm. high. $1,545

Rare engraved Jacobite goblet of seven petal design and air twist stem. $1,590

Fine goblet with pointed round funnel bowl, circa 1700, 7½in. high. $1,615

Bohemian ruby-flash goblet, bowl engraved with a jockey astride a galloping horse, circa 1845, 12.5cm. high. $1,680

Rare engraved Presentation goblet, 1824, 24.5cm. high. $1,855

Massive Dutch engraved goblet and cover, circa 1765, 47cm. high. $2,025

One of a pair of engraved glass goblets from the Imperial Glass Factory, 21cm. high, dated for 1911 and 1912. $2,025

16th century Venetian goblet, bowl with everted rim, 14.5cm. high. $2,040

Anglo-Venetian engraved armorial goblet of soda metal, late 17th century, 16cm. $2,070

Dutch engraved composite stemmed armorial goblet, circa 1750, 19.5cm. high. $2,365

Venetian goblet of the early 18th century, 10½in. high. $2,365

Saxon engraved goblet and cover with thistle-shaped bowl and facet-cut knopped finial, circa 1735, 44.5cm. high. $2,535

GOBLETS

German dated two-color goblet with thick-walled flared bowl, circa 1692, 20cm. high. $2,510

English goblet with a knop in the bowl enclosing a coin dated 1680, 17.2cm. high. $2,520

Baluster goblet with flared funnel bowl, circa 1700, 17.5cm. high.$2,700

Bohemian semi-translucent Lithyalin fluted goblet, circa 1840, 11cm. high. $2,880

Rare blue goblet, lightly fluted cup and plain stem, circa 1760, 16.5cm. high. $3,375

Early lead glass coin goblet, 10in. high, probably by Hawley Bishop, circa 1686. $4,050

Rare goblet, engraved with Frederick the Great and the double eagle of Prussia, circa 1757, 8¼in. high. $4,275

Arnsdorf blue overlay goblet engraved by G. J. Ostritz, circa 1860, 19cm. high. $4,330

Newcastle Dutch engraved Royal armorial goblet, circa 1745, 21.5cm. high. $4,370

110

A wheel-engraved Silesian goblet, made at Warmbrunn, circa 1760. $4,420

Early 17th century Facon de Venise glass goblet, 6¾in. high. $4,500

Facon de Venise Latticinio goblet, circa 1700. $4,500

Bohemian engraved and transparentemail goblet with hexagonal bowl, circa 1845, 12.5cm. high. $4,800

Dutch-engraved Newcastle marriage goblet with funnel bowl, circa 1760, 19cm. high. $5,235

Engraved Potsdam/Zechlin goblet, 6¼in. high, circa 1735. $5,850

Potsdam/Zechlin engraved mythological goblet, possibly by Johann Christian Bode, circa 1735, 21cm. high. $5,950

Engraved glass goblet from Dresden, circa 1730, 11¼in. high. $6,050

A goblet engraved with a three-master within the inscription 'Prosperity to the East India Company, Duke of Cumberland'. $6,440

111

GOBLETS

Engraved goblet in the manner of David Wolff, inscribed 'Iustitia', circa 1780, 18cm. high. $6,525

Thuringian marriage goblet by G. E. Kenckel, circa 1730, 20.5cm. high. $6,720

Royal Potsdam portrait goblet and cover, circa 1710, 13¼in. high. $7,425

Late 16th century Facon de Venise goblet, 10¼in. high, possibly Venetian. $7,875

Nuremberg engraved goblet and cover, circa 1680, 39.5cm. high. $13,050

An heraldic goblet decorated by Beilby of Newcastle, 8½in. high. $16,875

Unrecorded triple-portrait goblet, 1849, 15.5cm. high, engraved by Dominik Biemann. $19,125

18th century armorial goblet by William Beilby, 8in. high. $24,750

German goblet by Hermann Benkert, circa 1680, 20.5cm. high. $29,250

GLASS

GOBLETS

GOBLETS

Nuremberg Hausmaler Schwarzlot goblet decorated by J. L. Faber, circa 1700, 7¾in. high. $31,500

A magnificent Beilby armorial goblet inscribed 'W. Beilby Jr.', dated 1762, 8¾in. high. $56,250

Presentation goblet by Giacomo Verzelini, 1584, 6¼in. high. $180,000

HUMPENS

18th century German stangenglas, 8in. high. $270

19th century German marriage humpen with shaped base, 23.5cm. high. $285

Large late 19th century enameled humpen and cover, dated 1899. 49cm. high. $380

Late 19th century enameled humpen, 21.4cm. high. $720

Bohemian enameled humpen, circa 1590, 11½in. high. $16,875

Franconian enameled glass betrothal humpen and cover, 1615, 41cm. high. $32,625

113

GLASS

INKSTANDS

Victorian octagonal glass ink bottle. **$15**

Square shaped plated inkstand, with chased border and glass ink-well. **$35**

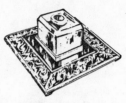

Victorian brass inkstand, circa 1850. **$35**

Victorian glass and marble inkstand. **$60**

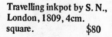

Travelling inkpot by S. N., London, 1809, 4cm. square. **$80**

A Victorian glass inkwell with a cat, circa 1860. **$115**

Lalique glass inkwell with domed body, 1920's, 16cm. diam. **$140**

A Stourbridge millefiori inkwell. **$340**

Lalique amber glass inkwell and cover, 1920's, 15.75cm. diam. **$790**

114

INKSTANDS

INKSTANDS

Art Nouveau glass inkwell depicting a lizard emerging from a pond. $1,690

A rare Tiffany inkwell depicting four frogs. $3,375

Clichy inkwell of hexagonal shape, with opaque turquoise ground, cover with gilt metal mount, 11.4cm. high. $4,165

JARS

Early light amber glass 'Bovril' jar. $5

Victorian cut glass pickle jar. $8

Victorian chemist's glass jar with 'Rhubarb' painted in gold and blue, 40ins. high. $175

A large apothecary's jar, made of crude bottle glass with enamel splatter. $190

Molded glass pomade jar in the form of a bear, Sandwich, Massachusetts, circa 1845, 3¾in. high. $200

Smith Brothers jar with opal glass body and plated silver top. $225

JARS

Victorian tobacco jar bearing 'The Jolly Japers'.
$340

Eglomise glass chemist's jar with St. George and the Dragon. $505

Albertine covered jar, New Bedford, Massachusetts, circa 1885. $525

Silver mounted glass jar and cover by W. C. Connell, London, 1901, 14.57cm. high.
$520

Stylish Oertel Haida enameled glass jar and cover, 23cm. high, circa 1905.
$540

Large glass chemist's jar with armorial transfer, English, circa 1890, 31in. high.
$540

Lalique 'Druids' opalescent glass jar, 10cm. diam. $670

19th century garniture of cut-glass covered jars with Dutch silver mounts. $790

One of a pair of apothecary jars marked 'Castor Oil Seeds' and 'Cassia', with original contents, 20in. high.
$790

18th century German enameled apothecary jar, 7in. high. $900

Rare red Pekin glass covered jar, decorated in relief with a dragon among clouds, 12.5cm. high. $1,080

18th century German enameled apothecary jar, 8¾in. high. $1,125

Unusual Galle enameled glass pot pourri jar, 30cm. high, circa 1890. $1,610

Late 17th century/early 18th century German enameled apothecary jar, 7½in. high. $1,675

Mount Washington Royal Flemish covered jar, 7in. high. $2,455

One of a pair of 18th century German apothecary jars, 7¼in. high. $2,590

4th century pear-shaped jar with indented base, 6in. high. $5,065

Mameluke enameled glass sweetmeat jar and cover. $41,250

JUGS

A green glass jug with waisted cylindrical body and folded rim, 7½ in. high. $15

Victorian dark blue slag glass jug, 5in. high. $20

Victorian purple slag glass jug with ribbed decoration. $25

Glass jug with a wrythen body and applied handle, circa 1800. $35

Victorian white slag glass jug with thistle decoration. $35

Victorian pink glass jug with an amber handle. $50

Victorian cranberry glass jug, 7½in. high. $55

Victorian cranberry glass jug, 14½cm. high. $60

Victorian ruby glass jug with applied white glass flowers, 10in. high. $65

Victorian cut glass jug with plated mounts. $65

Good quality 19th century green and clear cut-glass jug with a silver lip, 7in. high. $75

Late Victorian cranberry glass jug with frilled handle. $75

Victorian cranberry glass jug with ridged decoration, 6½in. high. $80

19th century Mary Gregory decanter jug. $105

A Lalique clear glass jug, the handle molded with berries and foliage, 21cm. high. $110

Mary Gregory glass jug, 8in. high. $115

A small Georgian cut-glass jug, 4½in. high, circa 1810. $125

Burmese glass jug, 4in. high. $165.

GLASS

JUGS

Mid 19th century Bristol clear glass jug. $165

Late Victorian ornamental jug, made at Stourbridge about 1880. $165

A mid 19th century Bristol clear glass jug. $165

French glass ale jug, circa 1790. $170

Enameled milchglas jug, Spanish or Bohemian, circa 1780, 19.3cm. high. $170

18th century Venetian cruet jug, 4¾in. high. $210

4th century A.D. pale green glass jug with strap handle, 3¾in. high. $250

Victorian Bohemian glass jug with red ground, 7in. high. $270

A good quality 19th century Loetz glass jug. $310

120

Glass lemonade jug with electroplated mounts, 1880's, 22.25cm. high. $310

A cut glass wine jug. $310

Cut-glass Irish jug with applied loop handle, circa 1820, 7¾in. high. $310

Clear glass jug attributed to Koloman Moser, in crackled and marble-veined glass, 18.7cm. high. $360

A silver mounted cut glass wine jug, German, circa 1860. $450

English ale jug, engraved with hops and barley and dated 1797, 7in. high. $450

Large pale green glass jug, with ovoid body, 2nd/3rd century A.D., 7½in. high. $495

Enameled and gilt milchglas jug and cover, 25.5cm. high, circa 1770. $520

Unusual glass jug of urn shape, circa 1820, 29cm. high. $745

JUGS

One of a pair of Water-
ford cut glass jugs.
$945

Roman jug, with bulbous
body, about 2nd century,
3in. high. $975

Daum mounted cameo
glass jug, neck with silver-
colored metal mount,
circa 1900, 23cm. high.
$980

Venetian jug, about 1640,
with dark turquoise rim
and pinched lip.
$1,125

A Guild of Handicrafts jug,
with a green body in a
silver frame, 8½in. high.
$1,690

Mid 16th century Venetian
gilt and enameled. jug,
8¾in. high. $2,025

Ravenscroft crisselled decanter jug with seven vertical
pincered and winged ribs,
with a replaced foot.
$2,815

A Ravenscroft syllabub jug,
gilt on sloping shoulders,
with the label 'Honey
Syllabub'. $9,000

Glass decanter jug
by G. Ravenscroft
with a heart-shaped
lid. $11,220

Victorian claret jug with tall panel cut neck, 34.5 cm. high. $80

Early Victorian ruby glass claret jug, circa 1840. $115

Late 19th century glass claret jug with plated mounts. $120

George III claret jug, circa 1820. $180

Victorian red glass claret jug with plated mounts. $210

Late 19th century German electroplated glass claret jug, 33.5cm. high. $255

Cut glass and silver claret jug, 1902. $360

Late 19th century silver mounted cut glass claret jug. $405

Silver mounted plain glass claret jug with rustic handle, by Charles Boyton, London, 1887, 27cm. high. $450

JUGS
CLARET

Silver mounted rock crystal engraved clear glass claret jug, by Wm. Comyns, London, 1899, 26cm. high.
$475

Walker & Hall silver mounted claret jug, London, 1883, 25cm. high.
$505

Mid Victorian claret jug in the form of a duck, with electroplate mounts, 14in. high. $530

German silver mounted clear glass claret jug, by David Kugelmann, late 19th century, 27.5cm. high.
$540

Silver plated glass claret jug by C. Dresser. $540

Cut glass claret jug London 1902. 11¼in. high. $570

Victorian frosted glass claret jug, with silver mounts. $575

Silver mounted cut glass claret jug by Lee & Wigfull, Sheffield, 1895, 27.5cm. high. $655

Silver mounted rock crystal engraved glass claret jug, Birmingham, 1894, 29cm. high. $695

Mappin & Webb silver mounted cut glass claret jug, London, 1902, 28.3cm. high. $720

Late Victorian glass claret jug, silver gilt handle and mount, maker F.B.M. London, 1887, 10in. high. $765

Mid Victorian claret jug, Sheffield 1877. $780

Silver mounted cut glass claret jug by W. & G. Sissons, Sheffield, 1899, 26cm. high. $900

Victorian silver mounted clear glass 'Lotus' claret jug, 7¼in. high, by E. H. Stockwell, London, 1880. $900

Joseph Rodgers & Sons silver mounted engraved cranberry flashed glass claret jug, Sheffield, 1875, 28.2cm. high. $945

Victorian cut glass claret jug with silver mount, Sheffield, 1871, 28cm. high. $1,015

Long necked silver mounted claret jug, made in London 1872 by E. C. Brown, 11½ in. $1,065

John Foligno claret jug, London, 1806. $1,180

125

JUGS
CLARET

Silver gilt mounted engraved glass claret jug, by R. Garrard, London, 1856, 28cm. high. $1,350

Silver mounted claret jug, made by James Powell & Son, London, 1904. $1,350

Silver mounted clear glass claret jug, by Hunt & Roskell, London, 1857, 34.5cm. high. $1,755

A French cameo glass claret jug by Daum, decorated with sprays of poppies and silver gilt mounts, 12½in. high. $1,800

Unusual Saunders & Shepherd silver mounted glass claret jug, London, 1895, 20.4cm. high. $1,845

Rare amber cameo claret jug with a plated mount. $1,980

An exceptionally fine Webb cameo glass claret jug. $2,250

Pair of 19th century claret jugs, the silver mounts representing the walrus and the carpenter, 15½in. long and 8¾in. high. $2,340

Victorian silver gilt mounted glass claret jug, 1899, 41.3cm. high. $3,375

Mary Gregory hand-painted glass cream jug. $35

Cut-glass cream jug, circa 1830. $90

Irish glass flat cut cream jug. $95

Irish glass yacht cream jug, circa 1800. $165

Lynn glass pear-shaped cream jug with everted rim and scroll handle, circa 1770, 9cm. high. $240

Nailsea baluster cream jug, clear glass with opaque white decoration, circa 1820, 9cm. high. $270

Early 18th century pear-shaped cream jug with clipped scroll handle, 9cm. high. $290

Late 17th century glass cream jug with clipped scroll handle, 9cm. high. $290

Cream jug of bell shape with wrythen molded lower part, circa 1720, 10cm. high. $335

WATER JUGS

Late Victorian plain glass water jug, 10in. high. $15

A heavy cut glass water jug, 11½ in. high. $35

Victorian glass water jug decorated with embossed flowers. $45

Victorian ruby glass water jug. $60

A heavy George III plain glass water jug. $75

Georgian cut glass water jug. $95

English water jug, with broad flute cutting, about 1840 8 in. high. $140

English water jug with cut swags, about 1820, 11ins. high. $215

Irish water jug, about 1790, impressed Cork Glass Co., round the pontil mark, 6 in. high. $1,440

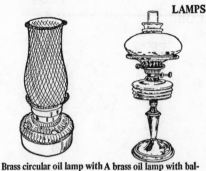

Crystal lamp with globular shade, 39.5cm. high. $55

Brass circular oil lamp with crimson glass shade, 20 in. high. $65

A brass oil lamp with baluster stem, white molded reservoir and shade. $90

Unusual plated oil lamp with a Nailsea chimney. $135

Pond lily table lamp in Art Nouveau style. $145

A brass circular oil lamp with crimson glass shade, 23 in. high. $165

Brass hall lantern with four leaded stained glass panels, circa 1860, 22 in. $165

19th century plated electric table lamp with a cut-glass shade. $200

Facon de Venise bird lamp, 9in. high. $200

129

GLASS

LAMPS

A 19th century cut-glass oil lamp, on circular base, with shade. **$215**

Czechoslovakian peach hanging chandelier, 1920. **$225**

Pairpoint fairy lamp with blown out pansy shade on wooden base. **$325**

Mid 18th century French lacemaker's lamp, 25.5cm. high. **$340**

Webb Burmese fairy lamp with floral decoration, signed. **$665**

Lithophane desk lamp with five panel shade, 15in. high. **$665**

Early 20th century cut glass lamp with detachable shade. **$700**

Walter pate de verre and wrought iron table lamp, 1920's, 31cm. high. **$810**

Art Deco table lamp by Daum of pink-tinted opaque glass, 20in. high. **$830**

130

A delicate fuschia lamp by Muller Freres, circa 1905. $830

Daum overlay lamp with purple and cloudy ground. $900

Favrile glass and gilt bronze desk lamp by Tiffany, 9¼in. high. $1,015

A Lalique table lamp in glass and iron. $1,080

Rare Webb's Burmese glass nightlight stand, circa 1887, 28cm. high. $1,285

Pairpoint table lamp with reverse painted 'Exeter' shade, 22in. high. $1,330

Small etched glass table lamp, attributed to Daum, 33.75cm. high, circa 1900. $1,400

Lalique lamp in frosted glass, 1920's, 10½in. high. $1,575

A fine late 19th century lamp by Muller. $1,650

131

LAMPS

Small Richard cameo glass table lamp base with Galle glass shade, circa 1900, 35cm. high.
$1,690

Bronze and Favrile glass linen fold floor lamp by Tiffany, 55in. high.
$1,690

Gilt bronze and Favrile glass three-light lily table lamp by Tiffany, 13in. high. $1,755

Galle glass table lamp, signed, about 1900, 35 cm. high. $1,910

One of a set of four Colza lamps on metal stands. $2,160

Lalique glass lamp, 1920's, 31.25cm. high.
$2,475

A Tiffany peacock feather leaded glass and gilt metal table lamp, 56cm. high.
$2,700

Wrought iron and glass floor lamp, circa 1945, 64½in. high.
$2,925

Tiffany lamp with a gilt bronze base and colored glass poppy pattern shade.$2,950

132

Tiffany Studio bronze table lamp with leaded glass shade, circa 1900. $3,375

Favrile glass and bronze bridge floor lamp by Tiffany, 55½in. high. $3,375

Daum cameo glass lamp, circa 1900, 44.5cm. high. $3,600

Tiffany Studio bronze table lamp. 34.5cm. high, 1910-20. $4,050

Tiffany lamp. $5,775

Bronze and glass standard lamp by Simon et Freres 6ft. 8ins. high. $5,900

Le Verre Francais cameo glass lamp with shouldered domed shaped shade, 1920's, 40.5cm. high. $6,300

Cut glass 'Gone with the Wind' lamp, signed L. Straus & Sons, 18½in. high. $6,430

Early Favrile glass and silvered bronze kerosene student lamp by Tiffany, 24in. high. $7,315

133

GLASS

LAMPS

Tiffany Studio bronze table lamp, circa 1900, 63cm. high. $8,100

Gilt bronze and Favrile glass twelve-light lily floor lamp by Tiffany, 55¼in. high. $11,700

Galle cameo glass lamp, circa 1900, 34.25cm. high. $12,375

An excellent Tiffany lamp. $13,350

Poppy leaded glass and bronze table lamp by Tiffany, 27¼in. high. $24,750

Galle cameo glass lamp, circa 1900, 52.5cm. high, in the form of a water-lily. $31,500

Daum glass lamp carved with marine motifs. $40,500

Tiffany Studio wisteria lamp. $48,000

Tiffany spider web lamp with bronze baluster base. $185,625

134

Victorian oil lamp shade of pink glass. $15

20th century painted glass hanging shade. $35

19th century Lithophane lamp shade on brass frame, 7¼in. $100

Lalique glass multiple panel hanging shade, 1920's, 49cm. diam. $745

Late 19th century American hanging leaded glass shade, 26¼in. diam. $750

Early 20th century Handel leaded slag glass hanging shade, 22½in. diam., Meriden, Connecticut. $800

Daum cameo glass lampshade, 31cm. diam, circa 1900. $2,700

Tiffany pendant colored glass lightshade, 28in. diam. $6,190

Yellow rose bush leaded glass hanging lamp by Tiffany, 24¼in. diam. $22,500

LIQUEUR SETS

An Art Deco Bristol glass
and metal decanter set,
Eastern United States,
circa 1927. $100

Black lacquer cocktail
set. $104

Victorian cut glass claret
jug and goblets. $150

Glass decanter and six glasses
with silver mounts and silver
overlay, circa 1920.
$225

A modernist cocktail service,
consisting of a decanter and
six glasses, circa 1930. $270

Decanter and six glasses
in stand, circa 1840.
$270

Modernist glass liqueur set
with tray, 1930's.
$305

Part of a liqueur set of a
clear and frosted glass
jug and ten glasses by R.
Lalique. $380

19th century Bohemian gilt
drinking set, jug 33.5cm.
high. $395

136

GLASS

Part of a liqueur set of a clear and frosted glass carafe and twelve glasses, by R. Lalique. $400

Electroplated mounted frosted and cut glass whisky barrel and tot, 1863. $475

Etched liqueur service in glass, 1930's. $495

Late 19th century blue glass decanter and six glasses, painted, silvered and gilt decorated.
$585

Part of a sixty-five piece gilt glass service. $870

American black wooden butler holding a rack with glasses, circa 1900, 48cm. high. $1,100

Good Moser glass set, circa 1900, in clear glass with floral decoration.
$1,240

Unusual liqueur set of oak, glass and silver, 57oz., London, 1881-82.
$4,500

Rare silver gilt and red lacquer water set, jug 28cm. high.
$10,100

137

LUSTRES

One of a pair of crimson Victorian lustres, circa 1880, 14in. high. $125

One of a pair of Bohemian overlay glass lustres, with cranberry glass body, 25cm. high. $160

One of a pair of 19th century overlay glass lustres, 12in. high. $270

One of a pair of ruby glass lustres with floral decoration and cut glass drops. $340

Portrait overlay lustre in green, circa 1850, 30cm. high. $355

One of a pair of early 19th century Regency cut glass lustres, 9in. high. $370

One of a pair of blue overlay lustre vases, circa 1850, 10½in. high. $710

One of a pair of overlay lustres in green and white, cut and enameled with flowers, circa 1850, 37cm. high. $775

One of a pair of ruby glass double lustres, about 1880. $955

MATCH-HOLDERS

Small Victorian glass shoe match-holder. $35

Glass match striker with silver container, Mappin Bros., 1896. $80

A Daum match-holder of rectangular form, the pale blue frosted glass body enameled with an Alpine scene, 4cm. high.
$225

MEAD GLASSES

Mead glass, bowl with honey-comb design molding , circa 1730, 11cm. high. $215

Early 18th century mead glass. $625

Opaque twist mead glass with cup-shaped bowl in-curved at the rim and gadroon molding on the lower half, 1750, 13.9cm. high. $730

A baluster mead glass with an incurved cup shaped bowl, circa 1710. $1,025

A 17th century English mead glass with a folded font. $1,135

Rare mead glass, 4¾in. high, circa 1700.
$1,915

139

MISCELLANEOUS

One of a pair of
St. Louis fruit
door handles, 2in.
$2,400

A John Henning glass paste
portrait medallion, 3¼in.,
signed Henning F., framed
and glazed. $215

A large glass sphere with
internal colorful trans-
fers on a white ground,
12 in. diam. $80

Victorian spun glass
house, 51 cm. high,
complete with glass
dome and wooden
stand. $360

Lalique glass hand
mirror, 1920's, 29.75
cm. high. $1,410

Bohemian ruby glass
flagon with ormolu
mounts, 11in. high.
$575

An unusual bird drinking
fountain bearing 'The
Kingfisher', 17.8 cm.
$800

Late 19th century two-
color glass compote,
European, 9¼in. diam.
$300

Early 20th century Tif-
fany gold iridescent pep-
per shaker, New York,
2¾in. high. $150

A small Mary Gregory amber glass pin tray depicting a boy with a butterfly net.
$190

Tassie glass paste medallion of A. Coventry M.D. of Edinburgh, 1794, 3½in., framed. $360

One of a pair of Victorian amber glass 'domes of silence'. $18

Dated St. Louis pen-holder, 1973, 13.6cm. high, set on a paperweight base. $270

Glass vessel, possibly Roman, 2nd century A.D., 8¾in. high. $49,500

Gilt and enameled opaline garniture, circa 1835, 14cm. high. $450

Victorian white slag glass spill holder. $25

Late 19th century Eastern United States two-colored cut-glass compote, 6in. diam. $175

Pale green Roman glass vessel in the form of a bucket, 13.7cm. high. $47,250

GLASS

MISCELLANEOUS

A large purple
hanging ball.
$55

Mid 18th century
Milchglas cane
handle, 3¾in.
high. $570

Victorian glass
mortar with lip.
$15

Art Deco dressing table
set, circa 1930.
$340

Daum glass and Brandt
wrought iron aquarium,
circa 1925, 148cm. high.
$3,065

One of a pair of glass but-
ter coolers, covers and
stands, 7in., circa 1790.
$970

Late 19th century
cut glass barrel with
a gun metal tap.
$80

One of a rare pair of 18th
century enameled opaque
white tureens, 4½in. high.
$790

Victorian glass ship
under a glass dome.
$290

Lalique square
clockcase, 4¼in.
square. $760

Victorian glass eyes. $25

Rare ormolu mounted
cameo glass wall flower-
bowl, 13in. diam.
$2,140

Lalique frosted and ena-
melled glass incense bur-
ner with chromed metal
fitment, 1930's, 13.5cm.
high. $305

17th century Venetian
reliquary, 14¼in. high.
$975

Two-handled jelly glass,
circa 1750, 10cm. high.
$295

Pedestal stemmed stand,
circa 1745, 12.5cm. high.
$135

Pressed glass miniature
covered tureen, Sandwich,
Massachusetts, circa 1828,
3in. long. $600

Bohemian rose water
sprinkler, circa 1850,
30.5cm. high.

$950

143

MUGS

Cut glass mug, circa 1820.
$115

Small dark brown Nailsea
mug, circa 1870, 6cm.
high. $155

Bottle glass beer mug with
white enamel splatter.
$190

Rare 18th century child's
glass ale mug finely
engraved with hops and
barley motif and the
inscription 'Cathleene',
4½ins. high. $240

Engraved coin ale mug of
bell shape, 6¾in. high.
$250

Glass mug with bulbous
lower part molded with
diamonds, circa 1730,
9.5cm. high. $290

One of a set of four Tiffany
iridescent glass mugs, circa
1900, 6.5cm. high.
$475

Rare Jacobite mug, 4¾in.
high, with ribbed applied
handle. $620

Bohemian milchglas mug
decorated with a roundel
enclosing a figure in
colored enamel, about
1750. $900

Newcastle plain stemmed wine glass of slender drawn trumpet shape, circa 1750, 18.5cm. high. $150

Engraved Newcastle friendship glass, 7¼in. high, circa 1750. $430

Engraved Newcastle wine glass, 7in. high, circa 1750. $690

Newcastle glass with a large slightly flared round funnel bowl, 9 in. high. circa 1745. $755

Engraved Newcastle glass, 7in. high, circa 1750. $865

Newcastle Dutch engraved wine glass, inscribed 'Hansie in de Kelder', circa 1750, 19cm. high. $930

Dutch engraved Newcastle wine glass showing a hen and her chicks, circa 1750, 18cm. high. $1,905

Dutch stipple engraved Newcastle wine glass. $3,375

18th century Newcastle wine glass. $6,185

145

PANELS

Late 19th century stained glass panel, Boston, signed W. J. McPherson-Boston, 15¼in. high. $425

German or Swiss stained glass panel showing a married couple, dated 1597, 33 x 24cm. $520

French stained glass panel showing the Risen Christ, dated 1542, 66 x 56cm. $585

15th century English stained glass roundel, 4½in. diam. $900

German polychrome leaded glass panel in oval mahogany frame, circa 1880, 165cm. high. $935

Late Victorian stained glass panel, one of a pair, 56in. high. $1,420

One of a pair of German stained glass panels, 16th century, 129.5cm. high. $1,690

Mid 16th century German sepia and yellow stained glass roundel, 9½in. diam., re-leaded. $3,825

16th century Italian verre eglomise picture, 4¼ x 3¼in. $4,725

Victorian glass paperweight depicting a view of Scarborough. $35

Side view of Sentinel, an avant-garde paperweight. $45

Side view of Vortex by Colin Terris depicts a whirlpool movement. $75

Modern Scottish paperweight by Perthshire Paperweights Ltd. $160

Stourbridge millefiori paperweight. $160

St. Louis dated carpet ground weight, 1972. $180

St. Louis dated dahlia weight, 1970, with certificate and box. $180

Clichy sulphide weight with 'crystallo-ceramie' bust of Queen Victoria, 3in. diam. $225

Baccarat miniature pansy weight, 1¾in. diam. $260

Clichy miniature posy paperweight, 2in. diam. $270

St. Louis marbrie salamander weight, 8.5cm. high, damaged. $270

St. Louis pear weight, naturalistically modeled, 8.5cm. wide. $275

PAPERWEIGHTS

Unusual Lalique glass paperweight, 1920's, 12cm. wide. $295

Amber flashed zooglophite paperweight engraved with a stag, 8cm. diam. $340

Clichy miniature posy weight, 1¾in. diam. $350

Clichy close-millefiori weight with tightly packed ground of canes, 7.8cm. diam. $355

Pinchbeck paperweight depicting a boar hunting scene, 3½in. diam. $405

Miniature Clichy patterned paperweight, 2in. diam. $430

Clichy concentric millefiori weight with outer red and white staves, 7.5cm. diam. $430

One of a set of twelve 20th century Baccarat sulphide zodiac weights, 7cm. wide. $475

Baccarat sulphide weight with portrait of St. Antoine, 2¾in. $450

St. Louis amber flash posy weight, 6.6cm. diam. $495

Baccarat patterned millefiori weight in clear glass, 7.7cm. diam. $525

St. Louis clematis and jasper-ground weight, 6.5cm. diam. $530

Clichy green color-ground weight set with four concentric rows of canes, 7.5cm. diam. $545

Baccarat mushroom weight with star-cut base, 7.8cm. diam. $570

Baccarat primrose paperweight, 6.5cm. diam. $585

Clichy patterned millefiori paperweight, 8.3cm. diam. $585

Baccarat dated close millefiori weight, 1849, 6.5cm. diam. $595

Baccarat anemone weight, 7.1cm. diam., with star cut base $605

Baccarat patterned millefiori weight set with white and coral pink canes, on star-cut base, 8.3cm. diam. $620

Baccarat mushroom weight on star-cut base, 8cm. diam. $640

St. Louis crown paperweight with alternate, white, translucent green and translucent red threads, 6.5cm. diam. $665

Daum pate de verre paperweight, 13cm. long, 1920's. $700

Modern but very rare Scottish paperweight by Paul Ysart, signed PY. $720

Baccarat pink double clematis paperweight with star-cut base, 8cm. diam. $735

149

PAPERWEIGHTS

Baccarat close millefiori paperweight, 6.5cm. diam. $775

One of a pair of Pinchbeck paperweights with portraits of Victoria and Napoleon. $790

Clichy swirl weight with alternate lime green and white staves, 7.5cm. diam. $800

St Louis pom-pom weight, 2in. diam. $865

Rare New England glass fruit weight, 3½in. wide. $865

St. Louis concentric millefiori mushroom weight on star-cut base, 7.5cm. diam. $865

Baccarat dog-rose weight, flower with white petals, 6.6cm. diam. $875

American sandwich paperweight with one deep pink flower with pointed petals. $890

St. Louis bouquet of fruit, set in a basket of white Latticinio. $900

Baccarat faceted pansy weight in purple and yellow, 7.3cm. diam. $910

Rare St. Louis butterfly paperweight, diamond-cut base, 7.5cm. diam. $920

Clichy swirl weight with pink and white pastry-mold cane, 3¼in. diam. $945

Clichy color-ground paper-weight, opaque turquoise-ground set with green canes, 8cm. diam. $950

Rare St. Louis blown pear weight, 6.5cm. square at base, slightly chipped. $950

Clichy faceted scattered mille-fiori weight with pink central rose, 7.2cm. diam. $960

Baccarat portrait weight of Queen Victoria, 3½in. $960

Clichy Barber's Pole paper-weight, signed 'C', 8.3cm. diam. $990

Baccarat double clematis and garland weight, 7.5cm. diam.$990

Rare pansy pedestal paper-weight, 5.5cm. high. $1,010

Clichy faceted patterned millefiori weight with central turquoise and white cane, 8cm. diam. $1,025

Clichy patterned millefiori weight in turquoise and white surrounded with pink, 6.5cm. diam. $1,025

Clichy swirl weight with alternate mauve and white staves, 7.5cm. $1,025

Baccarat glass millefiori paperweight, signs of zodiac, dated 1847. $1,070

Baccarat strawberry weight, clear glass enclosing a green leafy spray and two straw-berries, 7cm. diam. $1,070

PAPERWEIGHTS

St. Louis magnum crown newel post weight, 5½ins. high. $1,080

St. Louis double clematis weight, 7.5cm. diam. $1,115

Clichy paperweight with millefiori arrangement of two rows of florettes. $1,160

St. Louis crown paperweight with alternate twisted ribbons of white filigree, 6.8cm. diam. $1,190

Baccarat translucent green overlay weight with four concentric rows of canes, 6.7cm diam. $1,190

St. Louis mushroom paperweight, top and sides cut with printies, 7.5cm. diam. $1,235

Clichy turquoise 'barber's pole' concentric millefiori weight, 7.2cm. diam. $1,255

Baccarat 'shamrock and butterfly' paperweight, 8cm. diam. $1,265

Miniature Clichy pansy paperweight, 4.6cm. diam. $1,305

Clichy barber's pole paperweight, 7.2cm. diam. $1,380

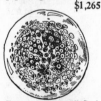

Rare patterned millefiori paperweight with seven clusters of canes, probably Clichy, 7.4cm. diam. $1,380

Close millefiori weight by Baccarat dated B1847. $1,390

Mid 19th century Clichy paperweight of a white dahlia with four leaves. $1,475

Baccarat faceted translucent blue-flash patterned millefiori paperweight, 7cm. diam. $1,520

A Baccarat millefiori paperweight. $1,590

Fine St. Louis upright bouquet paperweight, 7.5cm. diam. $1,590

Baccarat faceted turquoise-overlay patterned millefiori weight on star-cut base, 8cm. diam. $1,595

Lalique glass frog paperweight, 6.1cm. high, circa 1930. $1,640

A St. Louis upright bouquet paperweight, 7.5cm. diam. $1,660

Clichy color-ground sulphide paperweight, set with a crystalloceramie portrait bust, 7.3cm. diam. $1,665

St. Louis pom-pom weight on star-cut base, 7.5cm. diam. $1,665

Rare Baccarat translucent green ground weight, 3½in. diam. $1,690

St. Louis signed and dated mushroom weight, 1848, 7.3cm. diam. $1,825

Clichy garlanded posy weight, 6.7cm. diam. $1,825

153

GLASS

PAPERWEIGHTS

Very rare, Clichy 'crystallo-ceramie' weight, 3in. diam. $1,835

Rare fruit pedestal weight, clear glass set with a life-like peach, 6cm. high. $1,840

Baccarat butterfly and garland paperweight. $2,025

St. Louis 'crown' glass paperweight. $2,050

Good Clichy patterned millefiori weight, 3in. $2,050

Cut St. Louis concentric mushroom paperweight, in tones of white and blue, 7.3cm. diam. $2,070

Pate de verre chameleon paperweight by H. Berge in deep green glass, 1910, 8.6cm. high. $2,100

St. Louis pom-pom weight, 2¾in. diam. $2,105

Clichy patterned millefiori paperweight, 8cm. diam. $2,140

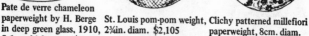

Rare Baccarat primrose weight with five rounded orange petals and stardust stamens, 2⅛in. $2,160

St. Louis fuchsia weight, 3¼ins. diam. $2,300

St. Louis 'crown' glass paperweight. $2,350

154

Rare Baccarat flat bouquet weight, 3in. $2,400

Clichy pansy flower delicately colored with leaves of pale purple and lemon.
$2,450

Signed St. Louis concentric millefiori paperweight with central dancing devil cane, 7.8cm. diam. $2,760

St. Louis cherry paperweight, 8.3cm. diam.
$2,925

Clichy moss ground concentric millefiori paperweight, 6.3cm. diam. $2,925

Baccarat double overlay paperweight, turquoise overlay and millefiori center, 8cm. diam.
$3,150

St. Louis carpet-ground paperweight, 6cm. diam.
$3,150

St. Louis faceted paperweight. $3,150

Baccarat butterfly and flower paperweight with star cut base, 7.5cm. diam.
$3,190

Baccarat paneled carpet-ground paperweight, 8cm. diam. $3,375

Baccarat wheatflower with pointed yellow petals and black markings. $3,425

Baccarat glass paperweight, rare because of its intricate work.
$3,425

155

PAPERWEIGHTS

St. Louis fuchsia paperweight. $3,600

Baccarat bellflower weight, 3in. diam., with star cut base. $3,600

St. Louis carpet-ground paperweight in salmon pink and blue with central bust of the Empress Josephine. $3,935

Rare Baccarat paperweight showing a butterfly hovering over a flower. $4,125

Rare, St. Louis magnum crown paperweight, 4in. diam. $4,500

Mid 19th century French paperweight by the Baccarat factory. $4,950

St. Louis green carpet ground paperweight.
$5,300

Rare Baccarat peach weight in tones of orange and green, on star-cut base, 7.3cm. diam.
$5,710

Scattered moss-ground paperweight, 6.7cm. diam. $6,425

Bouquet paperweight by Baccarat, superb quality and condition.
$6,600

Clichy glass bouquet paperweight identifiable by the pink ribbon tying the stalks. $6,600

St. Louis crown weight with spiral twisted ribbons. $7,000

Baccarat faceted double over-lay paperweight with colored garlands. $7,800

Rare, Clichy convolvus weight, 3in. diam. $8,100

St. Louis dahlia paper-weight, 8cm. diam. $9,000

Very fine Clichy moss-ground paperweight, 8cm. diam. $9,450

Clichy flat bouquet weight with central pink clematis. $11,000

Rare Baccarat butterfly and flower weight. $11,110

Rare Baccarat flat bouquet weight of two crossed sprays of clematis. $12,375

Very rare St. Louis cruci-form ground paperweight, 7.5cm. diam. $12,375

Clichy flat bouquet weight with shaded pink rose and white convolvus. $23,000

Clichy lily of the valley weight. $28,000

Rare Clichy convolvus bou-quet weight, 2¾in. diam. $81,000

Mid 19th century St. Louis paperweight in clear and colored glass, 8cm. diam. $108,000

GLASS

PIPES

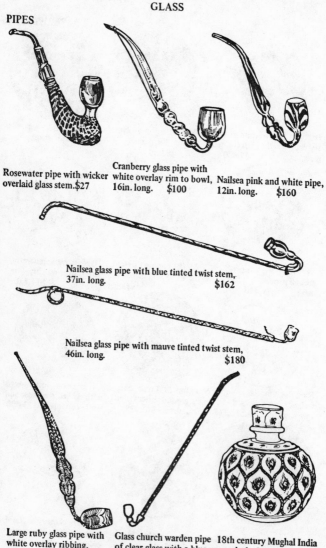

Rosewater pipe with wicker overlaid glass stem. $27

Cranberry glass pipe with white overlay rim to bowl, 16in. long. $100

Nailsea pink and white pipe, 12in. long. $160

Nailsea glass pipe with blue tinted twist stem, 37in. long. $162

Nailsea glass pipe with mauve tinted twist stem, 46in. long. $180

Large ruby glass pipe with white overlay ribbing, 28in. long. $185

Glass church warden pipe of clear glass with a blue bowl, 122cm. long. $170

18th century Mughal India vessel, the base of a hookah. $2,125

**Victorian amber
glass water pitcher
$55**

**Pressed glass water pitcher
with applied handle, 9¼in.
high. $150**

**19th century American
amberina conical water
pitcher, 8½in. high.
$175**

**Blown glass water pitcher
by Thomas Caines, South
Boston Glass Co., circa
1815, 6¾in. high. $350**

**Late 19th century Eastern
United States cut-glass
water pitcher, 14½in. high.
$575**

**Cased wheeling peach
blown pitcher, 5¼in.
high. $665**

**Late 19th century cut-glass
water pitcher, Eastern
United States, 6½in. high,
with sawtooth rim. $700**

**Galle carved glass pitcher
in smoked glass, 1890's,
15.5cm. long.
$1,240**

**4th century pale green glass
pitcher, slightly cracked,
12¾in. high.
$16,875**

PLAQUES

Baccarat sulphide glass cameo plaque of Charles X, 10cm. long. $340

An illuminated Lalique glass plaque carved with a naked archer, 4ins. diam. $1,450

A carved cameo amber glass plaque by Taid G. Woodhall, 16.5 cm. high. $5,000

Rare Lalique panel initialled L'oiseau Du Feu, molded in relief, 17in. high. $6,225

Lalique plaque depicting peacocks, sold with a similar piece. $6,750

Fine bronze mounted pate de verre plaque of Isadora Duncan, 17½in. high. $11,250

Art glass plaque by George Woodhall. $12,600

Webb cameo glass plaque carved by H. J. Boam, 1885. $16,875

Cameo glass plaque by George Woodhall, circa 1885. $34,500

Late Victorian frosted
pressed glass plate, 8in.
diam. $10

Victorian plate
commemorating
Gladstone. $25

19th century light blue
slag glass plate with basket
weave edge. $27

Late 19th century Tuthill
cut-glass plate, signed,
Middletown, New York,
8¾in. long. $350

Early 20th century Libbey
Glass salesman sample
cut-glass plate, Toledo,
Ohio, 6in. diam.$1,200

Venetian diamond engraved
Latticinio plate, late 16th
century, 16.5cm. diam.
              $1,800

PORTRAIT PLAQUES

Biemann portrait plaque
of oval form, circa 1830,
8cm. long, probably
Franzensbad.
           $10,800

Sulphide glass cameo
plaque of General Lafayette,
8.5cm. wide. $205

Sulphide glass portrait
plaque of George III, 10cm.
diam. $540

POTS

Dutch silver mustard
pot with glass liner.
$75

Lithyalin pounce-pot with
pewter mount, 2¾in. high.
$450

An iridescent glass
honey-pot. $470

Daum etched and applied
cameo glass pot and
cover, 12.5cm. high, circa
1910. $790

Silver mounted cameo
and applied glass pot
by Galle. $830

Unusual Pekin glass brush-
pot, thinly cased in red,
engraved mark of
Qianlong, 17.5cm. high.
$1,125

RANFTBECHER

Cut, stained and engraved
'Ranftbecher', circa 1840,
12cm. high. $405

One of a pair of gilt opalescent Ranftbechers,
Bohemian, circa 1830,
12.5cm. high. $910

Anton Kothgasser transparentemail Ranftbecher, Vienna, circa
1820, 11.5cm. high. $9,120

RATAFIA GLASSES

RATAFIA GLASSES

Ratafia glass with a narrow straight sided funnel bowl molded to two thirds of its height, circa 1745. $450

Rare Jacobite opaque twist ratafia glass with ogee bowl, circa 1765, 18cm. high. $600

Engraved ratafia glass, circa 1760, 7½in. high. $620

ROEMERS

17th century Rhenish roemer of light green tint, 14cm. high. $600

17th century Rhenish roemer of light green metal with concave bowl, 14.8cm. high. $630

17th/18th century Rhenish green tinted roemer, 15.5cm. high. $680

17th century Rhenish roemer of light green metal, 14cm. high. $945

17th century roemer of green-tinted metal with cup-shaped bowl, 15.3cm. high. $1,095

17th century Netherlandish green tinted roemer with cup shaped bowl, 20.5cm. high. $5,642

RUMMERS

A Georgian rummer glass. $35

A clear Georgian rummer. $40

Late 18th century rummer engraved with a gentleman fishing, 11.5cm. high. $60

Ale rummer engraved with hops and barley, circa 1880. $75

Engraved rummer of traditional shape with the initials S.J., 1800, 14cm. high. $110

Large engraved rummer, circa 1800, 7in. high. $145

Large engraved rummer, early 19th century, 8¼in. high. $170

Large ale rummer with lemon squeezer foot, circa 1810. $180

One of a pair of engraved masonic rummers, 6¼in. high, circa 1820. $215

164

Sunderland Bridge rummer, with the initials G.A.H., 1800, 12.7cm. high. $220

Rummer with bucket bowl engraved with a sailing ship under the Sunderland Bridge with the monogram M.J.G., 5½ins. high. $235

Sunderland Bridge rummer, 6½in. high, circa 1820. $290

Rummer engraved with a view of St. Nicolas' Church, Coventry, 1820, 15.2cm. high. $325

Battle of the Boyne commemorative rummer, 1690, 6in. high. $350

Engraved rummer, circa 1800, 5¼in. high, with lemon squeezer foot. $450

George III commemorative rummer, 1809, 8in. high. $640

Sunderland Bridge engraved rummer with bucket bowl, 8¾in. high. $745

Finely engraved armorial rummer, circa 1798, 6¾in. high. $900

SALTS

Small, Irish glass pair of salts. $60

One of a pair of Irish glass boat shaped salts, circa 1800. $145

One of a set of four William IV chased and pierced salts with blue glass liners. Sheffield, 1828. $470

SCENT ATOMISERS

Black glass perfume bottle with atomiser, 9.8cm. high. $70

Decorated glass atomiser, 10.5cm. high, circa 1920. $230

Lalique frosted glass scent atomiser, 13cm. high, 1920's $260

Lalique frosted and enamelled glass perfume atomiser, 1930's, 9.5cm. high. $270

Lalique frosted glass scent atomiser, 15cm. high, 1920's. $305

Lalique frosted glass scent bottle with metal atomiser fitment, 14cm. high, 1930's. $355

20th century cut glass scent bottle. $18

Edwardian bottle for lavender salts, with plated top. $25

Art Deco colored glass scent bottle. $35

Mid 19th century painted glass scent bottle.
                                    $36

Victorian ruby glass scent bottle with silver top. $45

Guerlain 'Mitsouko' glass bottle and stopper.
                                    $55

Cut glass perfume bottle with silver screw top by Aspreys, London, 1886.
                                    $55

Victorian Bristol blue scent bottle with embossed silver top. $60

19th century green scent bottle with a silver screw top.
                                    $60

SCENT BOTTLES

Molded glass perfume bottle and stopper, 1920's, 13cm. high. $65

Double ended blue glass scent bottle with silver gilt mounts. $65

Victorian vaseline glass scent bottle. $65

Scent bottle by G. & W., Birmingham, 1899. $75

Silver mounted cut glass perfume spray, 1899, 5in. high. $80

Art Nouveau silver and blue enamel perfume bottle, 2¼in. wide. $80

Cut crystal perfume bottle with silver top, 1898, 5in. high. $85

An Art Deco pink tinted, cut glass scent bottle. $85

One of two glass perfume bottles, 1920's. $85

19th century scent bottle in a pierced gilt metal mount inset with four landscape vignettes, 12cm. high. $90

Lalique glass scent bottle for Guerlain's 'Shalimar', 17cm. high, circa 1920. $90

Small Victorian gilt and enamel scent bottle. $110

Victorian vaseline glass scent bottle. $110

Victorian egg-shaped scent bottle, silver mount and cap, by Mappin Bros., Birmingham, 1887. $110

Blue glass scent bottle, late 19th century, with gilt metal mounts, 3½in. high. $115

Victorian blue and white overlay scent bottle. $125

Blue gilt and enamel scent bottle. $125

Lalique frosted glass scent bottle, 1920's, 12.5cm. high. $125

169

SCENT BOTTLES

Heart shaped scent
bottle on chain,
Chester 1888 $135

Amber glass bottle with
shaped stopper and silver
neck. $135

Mid 19th century
Bohemian glass
scent bottle. $145

Art Deco pagoda scent
bottle, 9in. high. $145

Green Bohemian glass
scent bottle with three
overlaid panels, 4.5ins.
high. $155

'Ivory cameo' scent bottle
in the form of a gourd,
circa 1890, with silvered
screw cap, 7.5cm. high.
              $155

Delvaux enameled scent
bottle and stopper,
1920's, 11.25cm. high.
              $170

Lalique clear glass scent
bottle, 13.5cm. high,
1920's. $175

Staffordshire opaque glass
scent bottle, 1770, 7.5cm.
high. $180

GLASS

Molded glass perfume bottle and stopper of triangular form, 1920's. $195

Pressed glass cologne bottle, Sandwich, Massachusetts, circa 1840, 6½in. high.. $200

Decorated clear glass perfume bottle and stopper, 13.75cm. high. $200

Lalique glass cologne bottle and stopper, 1930's, 17.5cm. high. $225

Molded glass perfume bottle and stopper, 12cm. high, 1920's. $250

Lalique glass scent bottle and stopper, 1930's, 11.7cm. high. $255

Lalique glass scent bottle, 1920's, 15.5cm. high, with frosted glass body. $260

Lalique frosted glass scent bottle, 12cm. high, 1920's. $270

One of a pair of Bohemian overlay scent bottles and stoppers of bell shape, circa 1860, 11.5cm. high. $285

SCENT BOTTLES

Burmese glass scent bottle
with silver screw cap,
circa 1885, 13cm. high.
$300

Mid 19th century Contin-
ental lithyalin cologne
bottle on pedestal base,
6in. high. $300

Bohemian glass scent
bottle of three layers,
10in. high. $300

One of a pair of ruby cased
scent bottles and stoppers,
circa 1850, 19.2cm. high.
$325

Bohemian scent bottle
with painted overlay and
gilt decoration, 19cm.
high. $325

Modernist glass bottle
and stopper, circa 1930,
26cm. high. $325

Gold mounted Venetian
scent bottle, 7cm. high,
mid 19th century. $360

Rare sulphide scent bottle
of flattened circular form,
7cm. diam. $370

Lalique glass bottle and
stopper of ovoid form,
1920's, 28.8cm. high.
$375

172

GLASS

Cameo glass scent
bottle with silver
stopper, 1885, 13cm.
high. $400

Lalique glass scent bottle
and stopper of swollen cylindrical form, 1930's, 8.7cm.
high. $405

Webb double overlay
globular scent bottle
and silver screw cover,
4in. high. $435

Victorian vinaigrette
cum scent bottle by
S. Mordan & Co.
          $450

A large early 18th
century gilded
glass scent bottle.
          $540

Cameo glass scent bottle
with hinged silver cap,
Birmingham, 1886, 12cm.
high. $585

Turquoise opaline ormolu
mounted scent bottle and
stopper of compressed
spherical form, circa 1830,
11cm. high. $585

Early 18th century German
silver and enamel scent
bottle, 3in. high.
          $595

One of a pair of Lalique
frosted glass scent bottles
and stoppers, 1920's,
9.2cm. high. $625

173

GLASS

SCENT BOTTLES

One of a pair of Lalique glass scent bottles, of square section, 1920's, 14cm. high. $630

Unusual Lalique glass multiple scent bottle, circa 1920, 22.5cm. long. $655

Tiffany iridescent glass perfume bottle and stopper, circa 1900, 11.5cm. high. $700

Daum scent bottle and stopper, 5in. high, signed. $700

Early Lalique glass perfume bottle with quatrefoil stopper, 1920's, 15.5cm. high. $700

Webb 'ivory' silver mounted scent bottle of tear drop form, circa 1885, 13cm. long. $735

Cameo glass scent bottle with silver cover and mount by Sampson Mordan & Co., London, 1887, 10.5cm. high. $765

Unusual St. Louis scent bottle, 6in. high. $790

Unusual Baccarat scent bottle, 5½in. high. $790

'Bleu ciel' opaline scent bottle and stopper decorated in silver and gilt, circa 1830, 11.5cm. high. $820

Double overlay cameo glass scent bottle by Thomas Webb & Sons, with silver top, 26cm. high. $830

Unusual St. Louis scent bottle in the form of a pear, 11cm. high. $855

Gilt metal and plique-a-jour enamel scent phial, 5.8cm. high, circa 1900. $945

George III silver cut glass scent bottle, 2¼in. high. $1,015

Lalique glass perfume bottle and stopper for Cyclamen by Coty, 1920's, 13.5cm. high. $1,030

A gilt enameled opaline scent bottle and stopper, circa 1830, 13cm. high. $1,125

Dutch glass scent bottle. $1,260

Clichy scent bottle and stopper with opaque turquoise ground set with red and white cane, 13.5cm. high. $1,310

SCENT BOTTLES

Ruby cameo glass scent bottle with silver hinged lid by Horton & Allday, Birmingham, 1887, 11.8cm. high. $1,330

Cameo glass scent bottle with silver cap by Horton & Allday, Chester, 1884, 23.8cm. long. $1,450

Early 20th century two-color cameo glass perfume bottle by Thomas Webb, 5¼in. high. $1,465

French or Italian double scent bottle, circa 1770, 4¾in. long. $1,580

Scent bottle by Tiffany. $1,800

Scent bottle with enamel case, 25mm. long. $1,915

Two amber ground cameo bottles, made by Thomas Webb, or Stevens & Williams. $2,800

Elegant scent bottle possibly decorated in London. $3,200

Clichy patterned millefiori scent bottle and stopper, 16.5cm. high. $3,400

French gold mounted clear glass scent flask with interior stopper, circa 1840, 10.1cm. high. $255

Silver mounted cut-glass fish scent flask by Sampson Mordan, 1884, 17cm. long. $375

One of a pair of Lalique scent flasks and stoppers of tapering square form, signed, 20.5cm. high. $380

Scent flask and smelling salts bottle by Sampson Mordan & Co., circa 1880, 7cm. high. $500

Frosted glass scent flask and stopper of tapering cylindrical form, by R. Lalique, 5in. high.$525

17th century German silver gilt scent flacon, 3½in. high. $780

Webb cameo glass, silver mounted, scent flask with silver cover, circa 1885, 18cm. long.$1,080

Unsigned Webb two-color cameo glass perfume flask, 7in. long, circa 1900. $2,000

Rare scent flask and stopper by Maurice Marinot, on spreading foot, 7½in. high. $2,320

SNUFF BOTTLES

Late 19th century interior-painted glass snuff bottle. $55

19th century red glass snuff bottle. $90

19tlr century glass interior painted snuff bottle. $100

19th century interior painted snuff bottle. $165

Interior-painted glass snuff bottle showing landscape scene, signed Bi Rongjiu, 1907. $180

A 19th century white glass snuff bottle with red overlay. $180

Interior-painted rock crystal snuff bottle and coral stopper, 2¾in. high. $215

Chinese opaque white glass overlay snuff bottle, red overlay, with coral glass and pearl stopper. $215

Red overlay glass bottle with jade stopper. $225

Chinese interior-painted glass snuff bottle with jade stopper, signed Yong Shoutian and dated 1924.
$225

Interior painted snuff bottle. $250

Blanc de chine snuff bottle carved with the Immortals, 2¼in. high. $350

Black overlay glass bottle with quartz stopper.
$385

Red overlay glass bottle, green glass stopper.
$385

Chinese opaque milk-white overlay glass snuff bottle, of blue and red overlay, with agate stopper.
$405

Pekin snuff bottle overlaid with red flowers.
$430

19th century Chinese glass snuff bottle, carved at the shoulders and with a coral stopper. $450

Famille rose Pekin glass bottle, with jade stopper.
$450

179

SNUFF BOTTLES

Chinese overlay
snuff bottle. $470

Chinese interior-painted
glass snuff bottle, with jade
stopper, signed Zhou
Leyuan. $540

Carved chalcedony
snuff bottle with
a russet inclusion.
$560

Early interior
painted Chinese
snuff bottle. $575

Unusual interior
painted snuff
bottle. $650

Chinese semi-translucent
overlay glass snuff bottle,
red overlay on 'snow-
storm' ground.$675

Interior-painted snuff bottle
by Ten Yu-t'ien.
$700

A Chinese glass snuff
bottle painted on the
inside with horses.
$760

Chinese overlay
snuff bottle.
$790

Early Chinese
snuff bottle.
$900

A fine 18th century
red overlay snuff
bottle. $1.080

An opaque turquoise snuff
bottle, the white and black
double overlays carved in
high relief, 2½ins. high.
$1.140

Disc-shaped opaque white
bottle, brilliantly enameled,
in colors in the Ku Yueh
Hsuan style, 2¼ins. high.
$1,440

Enamelled glass snuff bottle
of double gourd form, with
Qianlong mark, probably
from the Ye family kilns,
circa 1900.$2,925

A Qianlong Pekin ena-
mel snuff bottle painted
in famille rose colors.
$3,475

A rare portrait snuff
bottle by Tzu I-tzu,
the reverse side bearing
an inscription. $4,000

A rare interior-painted
glass snuff bottle of flattened upright form,
signed T'ing Yu-Keng,
dated 'Winter month,
1904'. $6,750

Rare enameled glass snuff
bottle by Ku Yueh Hsuan.
$13,800

TANKARDS

Pressed glass ale can with geometric decoration, circa 1860. $25

Glass tankard with initials B.H., W.S., circa 1825. $135

Early 18th century glass tankard with ribbed everted rim and applied scroll handle, 13.5cm. high. $155

19th century Mary Gregory sapphire blue tankard, 6½ins. tall. $210

Enameled milchglas tankard, Spanish or Bohemian, circa 1780, 13.2cm. high. $225

Bell-shaped glass tankard, with reeded scroll handle, circa 1760, 11.5cm. high. $265

Large glass tankard with scalloped foot, 6in. high, circa 1750. $270

One of a pair of Central European enameled milchglas miniature tankards, 3¼in. high, circa 1750. $325

Gilt amethyst-tinted tankard, cylindrical body inscribed in gilt, circa 1800, 5½in. high. $335

Central European enameled tankard, circa 1750, 5¾in. high. $445

Central European milchglas enameled tankard, 5½in. high, circa 1750.
        $485

Fine Central European enameled milchglas tankard, circa 1750, 6½in. high. $490

Bohemian cut glass souvenir tankard and cover, circa 1840, 25cm. high.
        $495

19th century Bohemian silver mounted amber flashed tankard with strap handle, Birmingham 1899, 29cm. high.
        $565

Humorous German engraved tankard, 4¾in. high, circa 1810. $605

Enameled milchglas tankard, Bohemian, circa 1770, 12cm. high.
        $645

Large engraved ale tankard with bell bowl, circa 1760, 20cm. high.
        $720

Central European enameled glass tankard with pewter lid and foot rim, 18th or 19th century, 24cm. high.
        $765

TANKARDS

German dated and
engraved tankard, 6½in.
high, circa 1739. $805

Ruby glass tankard with
silver hinged cover, 8in.
high. $920

Mid 18th century Central
European enameled tan-
kard in milchglas, 4½in.
high. $965

Unusual hunting overlay
tankard, circa 1850,
16.5cm. high.
          $990

Mid 18th century
engraved glass
tankard. $1,080

Central European enameled
tankard and cover, circa
1750, 24cm. high. $1,350

Mid 18th century German
engraved pewter mounted
tankard, 9½in. high.
          $2,140

Viennese enamel and rock
crystal flagon, 19.1cm. high,
circa 1890. $3,745

Rare Bohemian enameled
blue glass tankard, 6¼in.
high, circa 1608.
          $12,375

GLASS

TANTALUS

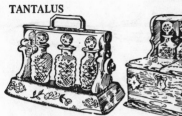

Small Victorian tantalus with three molded glass bottles. $250

Oak decanter box, circa 1880, with Bramah lock, 13¾in. wide. $475

TANTALUS

Victorian coromandelwood and brass tantalus with three bottles, 12in. wide. $620

TAPERSTICKS

Pedestal stemmed taperstick, 5½in. high, circa 1730. $270

Glass taperstick on domed and terraced foot, circa 1740, 5½in. high. $485

Unusual taperstick, 5½in. high, circa 1740. $540

Early English taperstick, circa 1700, 13.5cm. high. $810

One of a pair of South Staffordshire opaque white glass tapersticks and enamel drip-pans, circa 1760, 18.5cm. high. $900

A rare taperstick, the nozzle set on inverted baluster air twist stem, 6½in. high. $1,125

185

GLASS

TAZZAS

19th century Silesian stemmed small glass tazza, 3½in. high. $115

Small baluster tazza, with vertical gallery supported on two cushion knops, circa 1730, 11cm. diam. $215

Bohemian glass tazza, the shallow dish decorated with white threads, 9.5cm. high. $260

Small 'bleu lavande' opaline tazza, shallow bowl with border of gilt foliage, circa 1830, 9.5cm. diam. $310

17th century Venetian tazza, 2in. high, 6¼in. diam. $405

'Opale' opaline ormolu mounted two-handled tazza, bowl surmounted by two eagles, circa 1830, 23cm. wide. $525

'Opale' opaline ormolu mounted two-handled tazza, foot chased with a pin cushion pattern, 20.5cm. wide, circa 1830. $700

17th century Latticino tazza, 8in. diam. $725

Ormolu mounted opaline tazza, circa 1830, 13.5cm. high, with scroll handles surmounted by swans. $735

186

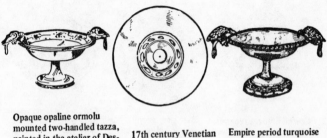

Opaque opaline ormolu mounted two-handled tazza, painted in the atelier of Desvigne, circa 1830, 21cm. wide. $740

17th century Venetian tazza, 8in. diam. $900

Empire period turquoise verne opaline mounted tazza. $975

Unusual 18th century set of five graduated tazzas. $1,035

'Gorge de Pigeon' opaline ormolu mounted two-handled tazza, compressed bowl with flared rim, circa 1830, 19cm. wide. $2,925

16th or 17th century Facon de Venise tazza, 22.5cm. diam. $3,150

Ormolu mounted amethyst and opaline tazza, circa 1830, 11cm. high. $3,375

Venetian filigree tazza, circa 1600, 6¾in. diam. $6,750

Late 16th century Facon de Venise enameled glass tazza, 5.9in. high. $9,450

GLASS

TEACUPS

TEAPOTS

Central European enameled milchglas teapot and cover, 6½in. high. $520

Rare glass globular teapot and cover, circa 1725, 15cm. wide. $770

Central European opaque opaline globular teapot and cover, mid 18th century, 16cm. wide. $790

TOASTING GLASSES

Drawn stem English wine glass, 7ins. high. $180

Incised twist toasting glass of drawn trumpet shape, circa 1755, 16.5cm. high. $425

Baluster toastmaster's glass, thick conical bowl, supported on a quadruple annulated knop, circa 1725, 13.5cm. high. $430

Air twist toasting glass of drawn trumpet shape, circa 1750, 19cm. high. $430

Toasting glass of slender drawn trumpet shape, circa 1750, 21.5cm. high. $430

Toasting glass of slender drawn trumpet shape on conical foot, circa 1750, 19.5cm. high. $475

Victorian cranberry glass tumbler. $20

'Last drop' ale tumbler, circa 1870. $90

Bohemian tumbler of almost thistle shape with engraved oval panel, circa 1850, 16.4cm. high. $110

Georgian tumbler inscribed 'The Independence of Durham' and 'Rich'd Wharton its Defender', 4ins. high. $125

Farmer's tumbler with agricultural emblems and the motto 'Speed the Plough', circa 1820. $125

Georgian tumbler with a pale blue rim inscribed Mary Fogg, with figures of Faith, Hope and Charity, 3½ins. high. $165

18th century Bohemian cut and engraved glass tumbler, 4¼in. high. $165

Blue flared tumbler, gilt by William Absalon, circa 1790, 11.5cm. high. $195

Georgian tumbler engraved 'Success to Change Ringing', 4ins. high. $200

189

TUMBLERS

Naval tumbler engraved with anchors, 4½in. high, circa 1800. $210

Glass tumbler of bell shape with everted rim, circa 1760, 11.5cm. high. $215

19th century engraved fox-hunting tumbler, 4in. high. $250

Extremely rare Jacobite engraved tumbler, 4¾in. high. $360

Baccarat tumbler, cylindrical body with molded panels and central oval cartouche enclosing a pink rose, 9.8cm. high. $430

One of a set of three Saxon tumblers, 4in. high, circa 1750. $490

Engraved glass tumbler, 4¾in. high, circa 1790. $490

Bohemian amber flashed tumbler of thistle shape, circa 1850, 14cm. high. $495

Bohemian tumbler engraved with cupids and allegorial scenes, circa 1730, 10.2cm. high.$495

GLASS

Turquoise opaline flared tumbler on circular foot, circa 1830, 8.5cm. high. $585

Bohemian dated tumbler with leaf-cut base, 1834, 12cm. high. $605

Engraved Bohemian tumbler, 5in. high, circa 1700. $630

North Bohemian armorial cylindrical tumbler on star cut base, circa 1810, 11.5cm. high. $640

Baccarat tumbler, body with molded panels around an oval cartouche with flower and butterfly, 8.8cm. high. $690

Baccarat tumbler, oval cartouche enclosing an enameled spray of flowers, 9.2cm. high. $690

Bohemian tumbler engraved with cupids, circa 1730, 10cm. high. $765

Early 19th century engraved tumbler, probably by Kugler-Graveur, 10cm. high. $810

Georgian Glass pint tumbler engraved with a coach and four, 10.2cm. high. $815

TUMBLERS

Late 17th century Bohemian Jagd flared tumbler, 11cm. high. $900

Cut glass Baccarat tumbler with enameled figure of Napoleon, 9.4cm. high. $900

Engraved Bohemian tumbler, 4¼in. high, circa 1700. $920

Small clear glass Silesian tumbler, 3¼in. high, circa 1725. $1,070

Unusual 18th century Spanish tumbler, 12cm. high. $1,090

Austrian armorial cut glass cylindrical tumbler, circa 1835, 9cm. high. $1,125

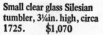

Venetian enameled tumbler, 18th century, 4½in. high. $1,295

18th century German, enameled glass tumbler, 12cm. high. $1,380

18th century engraved Central European tumbler with flared sides. $1,545

GLASS

Fine engraved commemorative tumbler, 3¾in. high, circa 1807. $1,800

A fine Mildner tumbler. $1,860

A rare Jacobite portrait tumbler with a portrait of the Young Pretender. $1,860

Bohemian amber flashed hexagonal tumbler, circa 1850, 14cm. high, with engraved sides. $2,140

Baccarat armorial tumbler with enameled coat of arms, 9.5cm. high. $2,700

Early Jacobite portrait tumbler engraved with a bust portrait of the Young Pretender. $3,940

URNS

One of a pair of large cut urns and covers, 12½in. high, circa 1790. $270

One of a pair of large covered urns, circa 1850, 46cm. high. $610

Engraved miniature glass urn and cover, 18th/19th. century, 15cm. high. $715

GLASS

VASES

Victorian red glass spill vase. $15

Victorian opal glass vase, 3½in. high. $15

Victorian glass spill vase, 7in. high. $15

Victorian orange carnival glass vase, 10in. high. $20

Slim Art Nouveau vase in pale blue glass. $25

Victorian opaline glass vase with flared rim. $30

Iridescent green blue vase with tear drop decoration. $30

Victorian opal glass vase, 10in. high. $35

Three handled Art Nouveau glass vase in green. $35

GLASS

VASES

Late 19th century irides-
cent vase with applied decoration, 5½in. high. $35

Edwardian celery vase
engraved with ferns.
26cm. high. $60

19th century baluster
vase in iridescent mauve
and green. $75

One of a pair of Victorian
colored glass vases
decorated with flowers.
10ins. high. $75

Dark green Art Nouveau
rippled glass vase in a
brass case with lily pad
design. $80

Bubble glass vase painted
with a 19th century mili-
tary scene. $85

Art Nouveau vase
decorated with
snails in fiery orange
and silver blue. $95

19th century American
amberina vase of baluster
shape, 9¾in. high. $100

One of a pair of 19th
century ruby and
decorated glass vases.
                    $110

195

VASES

A balustroid vase in iridescent blue green, 7¾ins. high. $125

One of a pair of Victorian opal glass vases, 10in. high. $125

One of a pair of Art Nouveau silver overlay blue vases. $135

Green glass tulip vase with blood red at the tips of the petals. $135

Art Nouveau glass vase in pale lime green with brown bullrushes rising from the base. $150

Late 19th century Eastern United States cut-glass vase, 10in. high. $155

Satin glass mother-of-pearl vase, America, circa 1880, 7in. high. $175

Pair of Art Nouveau blue cameo vases, 10in. high. $195

Late 19th century Roman style glass vase with spiral decoration. $215

Portrait overlay vase with tulip bowl, circa 1850, 45.4cm. high. $235

One of a pair of gray glass baluster vases, 18¼in. high. $270

Wheeling peachblow vase, West Virginia, circa 1890, 8¾in. high. $275

One of a pair of blue overlay glass vases, circa 1850, 38.5cm. high. $295

Late 19th century cut glass flower vase, American, 20cm. high. $300

Victorian overlay glass with portrait medallion, 14in. high. $300

Amberina glass vase bulbous body, circa 1890, 18cm. high. $300

18th century Pekin translucent deep red glass bottle vase, 24cm. high. $305

One of a pair of opaline overlay pink vases, with gold arabesques and polychrome floral decorations, 11ins. high. $310

197

VASES

Late 19th century peach-bloom bottle vase with tall cylindrical neck, 23.5cm. high. $315

One of a pair of gilt bronze and glass vases, 11in. high, circa 1880. $315

One of a pair of pink ground enameled opaline vases, circa 1850, 36cm. high. $350

One of a pair of ruby glass portrait overlay vases, circa 1850, 29.9cm. high. $370

Late 19th century Eastern United States cut-glass flower center in Harvard pattern, 7½in. diam. $375

One of a pair of cut glass vases, circa 1850, 59.2cm. high. $400

Orrefors engraved glass vase, 18.75cm. high, 1940's, sold with another. $405

Pressed glass vase in canary yellow, Sandwich, Massachusetts, circa 1840, 5¾in. high. $425

Spanish four-handled vase of bluish opalescent glass, early 18th century. $430

One of a pair of 18th century Venetian vases. $430

One of a pair of mid 19th century enamelled 'moonstone' vases, 29.5cm. high. $450

One of a pair of ruby overlay vases, circa 1850, 25.2cm. high. $475

One of a pair of mid 19th century enameled vases, 37.8cm. high. $475

One of a pair of Venetian 'bleu de roi' glass vases, early 20th century. $475

Late 19th century peachbloom vase of slender pear shape, 32cm high. $510

One of a pair of portrait overlay green glass vases, circa 1850, 33.8cm. high. $540

18th century royal blue bottle vase, 9in. high. $540

Late 19th century cameo glass vase, 22.5cm. high. $575

GLASS

VASES

Opaque opaline ormolu mounted two-handled vase on square ormolu base, circa 1830, 37cm. high. $585

18th century powder blue vase, 9½in. high. $600

Pressed glass vase in emerald green, Sandwich, Massachusetts, 1835-45, 10in. high. $600

New England peach blown lily form vase, 18in. high. $605

Portrait overlay vase in ruby glass with enamel decoration, circa 1850 42.5cm. high. $615

Rare cameo vase with white relief on a green ground, 16cm. high. $630

18th century pale blue ground bottle vase, 8¾in. high. $630

Opaline campana vase of lemon-yellow tint with gilt rims, circa 1860, 43cm. high. $740

One of a pair of amethyst giant thumbprint vases, Sandwich, Massachusetts, circa 1850, 10½in. high. $775

One of an unusual pair of glass bottle vases, each with an interior painting, 34cm. high, with wood stands. $795

Enameled opaline glass vase with flared neck, circa 1850, 44.4cm. high. $870

One of a pair of gilt and enameled overlay vases and covers, circa 1850, 38.8cm. high. $945

Pate de verre small oviform vase, 3¼in. diam. $900

Red overlay glass vase of 18th century origin. $970

Very rare miniature opaque white globular vase, 2½in. high, circa 1770. $1,170

One of a pair of flower encrusted bottle vases. $1,170

One of a pair of English white overlay glass vases, circa 1870, 12½in. high. $1,045

Late 17th century German vase mounted in copper and gilt, 8½in. high $1,160

VASES

One of an unusual pair of glass vases, circa 1880, 24.5cm. high.
$1,240

One of a pair of green overlay glass vases with flared mouths, circa 1860, 45cm. high. $1,330

Royal Flemish vase in mustard yellow with ruffled rim, circa 1889.
$1,400

A cameo glass vase of smokey quartz color, 9.5cm. high. $1,500

Royal Flemish glass modified stick vase, circa 1889, 33cm. high.
$1,500

Green tinted vase with gilt metal mounts, 17th century, 6½in. high.
$1,530

An escalier de cristal ormolu mounted cameo vase, 16.5cm. high.
$1,620

Good piece of Art Nouveau glassware with applied floral decoration.
$1,630

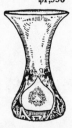

One of a pair of Austrian iridescent overlaid glass vases, 23cm. high, circa 1900. $1,915

Raisin-colored cameo vase, 30.5cm. high. $1,965

Enamelled opaque-white vase painted with flowers, possibly Tyneside or London, circa 1770, 6¾in. high. $2,140

18th century blue glazed baluster vase, 21½in. high. $2,585

One of a pair of turquoise opaline ormolu mounted two-handled oviform vases, necks with everted rims, 34cm. high. $2,730

One of a pair of opaline glass vases with flowers in colors on a turquoise ground, 39.5cm. high. $3,060

One of a pair of yellow ground cameo glass vases, 1880's, 30.1cm. high. $4,050

Rare Venetian diamond engraved vase, late 17th century, 11in. high. $4,275

Late 16th century Venetian mold-blown oviform vase, 9in. high. $4,950

A Victorian four-color oviform vase. $5,450

VASES
ARGY ROUSSEAU

Argy Rousseau pate de cristal vase, 14.75cm. high, 1920's. $1,240

An Argy Rousseau pate de verre oviform vase, 14.5cm. high. $5,175

Pate de cristal Argy Rousseau vase, 10in. high. $8,325

BOHEMIAN

Bohemian amber vase with hexagonal bowl engraved with deer and hounds, 20.3cm. high. $220

One of a pair of 19th century red colored Bohemian glass vases. $300.

One of a pair of Bohemian glass overlay vases, 19.7cm. high. $570

One of a pair of Bohemian gilt and enameled overlay vases, 17¼in. high. $990

19th century Bohemian cut opaline glass vase, 7½in. high. $1,000

One of a pair of Bohemian green and gilt vases, 17in. high. $1,440

DAUM

Large early 20th century Daum Nancy mottled glass vase, France, 12in. diam. $225

Signed Daum Nancy vase in orange, cream and green, 6½in. high. $250

Daum etched and enamelled glass vase, circa 1900, 8cm. high. $450

Daum cameo glass landscape vase, circa 1900, 18.75cm. high. $485

Daum etched and gilt 'vase pariant', circa 1900, 26cm. high. $790

Daum Nancy cameo glass vase, signed, circa 1900, 11¼in. high. $900

Daum etched and wheel carved cameo glass vase, circa 1900, 20cm. high. $1,125

Daum etched, carved and enameled glass vase, circa 1900, 13.5cm. high. $1,350

Daum cameo glass vase of teardrop form, 30.25cm. high, circa 1900. $1,350

**VASES
GALLE**

Miniature cameo vase, Galle. $170

A Galle cameo glass vase of uniform shape, the gray orange body overlaid in orange, 9cm. high. $215

A Galle cameo small baluster vase, the olive green body overlaid in darker green. $280

Miniature Galle cameo glass solifleur vase, 13cm. high, circa 1900. $360

Small Galle cameo glass vase, circa 1900, 8.5cm. high. $445

Galle cameo glass vase, after 1904, 17.5cm. high. $445

Small Galle cameo glass vase, 9cm. high. $450

A fine Galle vase, signed. $485

Galle cameo glass landscape vase, circa 1900, 11.75cm. high. $595

Small slender Galle cameo glass vase, circa 1900, 12.75cm. high.
$595

Galle cameo glass vase, circa 1900, 19.5cm. high.
$655

Galle cameo glass vase with ovoid body, 12cm. high, circa 1904. **$665**

Galle overlay oviform vase, 7½in. high, signed.
$675

Galle cameo glass vase with irregular rim, circa 1900, 13.25cm. high.
$700

Galle cameo glass mountainscape vase, 12cm. high, circa 1900.
$700

Galle cameo glass vase, circa 1900, of flattened teardrop form. **$780**

Galle cameo glass vase of hexagonal design, circa 1900, 21.5cm. high. $830

Galle cameo glass landscape vase, after 1904, 36cm. high.$945

VASES
GALLE

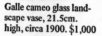

Galle cameo glass land-
scape vase, 21.5cm.
high, circa 1900. $1,000

Galle cameo glass vase,
13.75cm. high, circa
1900. $1,000

Galle, etched and carved
glass vase, 14.75cm. high,
1890's. $1,015

Galle cameo glass vase,
46.5cm. high, after
1904. $1,195

Galle cameo glass vase
and stopper, circa 1900,
20.5cm. high.
          $1,195

Galle cameo glass vase,
circa 1900, 36cm. high.
          $1,250

Galle cameo glass vase,
25.5cm. high, circa
1900. $1,275

Galle, etched and carved
cameo glass vase, 19.5cm.
high, circa 1900.
          $1,295

Galle cameo glass vase,
with inverted rim, 20.75cm.
high, circa 1900. $1,330

208

Galle cameo glass vase, circa 1900. 39.5cm. high. $1,350

Galle boat-shaped cameo glass vase, 19cm. wide, circa 1900. $1,385

Galle cameo glass vase, overlaid in brown, 43.5cm. high. $1,440

Galle carved glass vase, 28cm. high, 1890's. $1,445

A Galle enameled three-handled vase in the Persian style, 15cm. high. $1,465

Galle cameo glass 'vase de tristesse', 15.5cm. high, circa 1900. $1,610

Galle marine cameo glass vase, circa 1900, 23.5cm. high. $1,752

Galle cameo glass vase, circa 1900, 22cm. high, with boat-shaped rim. $1,755

Internally decorated Galle cameo glass vase, circa 1900, 13.5cm. high. $1,800

VASES
GALLE

Unusual Galle glass vase, circa 1900, 36.7cm. high, in mottled mauve and yellow glass. $1,848

Large Galle cameo glass vase, circa 1900, 50.75cm. high. $1,885

Galle cameo glass vase in amber, 49cm. high, circa 1900. $1,940

Large Galle landscape cameo glass vase, 44.25cm. high, circa 1900. $2,360

Good Galle cameo glass vase, 19.5cm. high, circa 1900. $2,925

Good, etched and carved Galle cameo glass vase, 18.25cm. high. $2,925

A Galle cameo tapering oviform vase with inverted quatrefoil rim, 35cm. high. $2,070

Large Galle double overlay square vase, 13¾in. high. $2,160

Mounted Galle cameo glass vase, circa 1890's, 7.75cm. high. $2,250

Good etched and carved Galle cameo glass vase, 18.25cm. high. $3,050

A Galle cameo and marquetry glass vase with silver mounts by Cardeilhac. $3,330

Good Galle cameo glass vase, 19.5cm. high, circa 1900. $3,605

A fine and rare marquetry vase by Emile Galle, made in 1900. $8,250

Large Galle cameo glass landscape vase, circa 1900, 63cm. high. $9,225

Glass vase by Emile Galle, with an applied decoration of a glass rose, around 1900. $13,500

Large Galle 'blow-out' glass elephant vase, circa 1900, 38cm. high. $24,750

A superb and very rare glass vase, by Emile Galle, 11¾in. high. $51,750

Internally decorated, carved and applied glass vase by Emile Galle, 1900, 23.2cm. high. $59,400

GLASS

VASES
LALIQUE

Lalique frosted glass vase, 1930's, 17.75cm. high. $180

Lalique frosted glass vase, 1930's, 15.5cm. high. $215

Lalique frosted glass vase, relief molded, 1930's, 13.5cm. high. $225

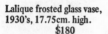

Mid 20th century Lalique frosted glass vase, 16.75cm. high. $225

Lalique frosted glass vase, 1930's, 15.25cm. high. $225

Lalique frosted glass vase, 17.5cm. high, 1930's. $250

Lalique opalescent glass vase, 22.75cm. high, 1920's. $260

A Lalique flared vase of matt glass and graduated form, 15.5cm. high. $290

Squat Lalique frosted glass vase, 17.75cm. high, 1930's. $290

GLASS

Mid 20th century Lalique frosted glass vase, 19.5cm. high. $290

Lalique frosted glass vase depicting two doves, signed, 1930's, 24cm. high. $350

Lalique globular vase of bluish tint, 6½in. high. $350

Lalique smoked glass vase, 11.5cm. high, 1920's, of flattened spherical body. $385

Lalique opalescent glass vase, 1930's, 22cm. high. $430

Lalique opalescent glass vase, 1930's, 18.75cm. high. $430

Deep red Lalique vase with globular body, slightly damaged. $450

Lalique blue glass vase, signed, 6in. high. $475

Heavy Lalique frosted glass vase, 1930's, 25.5cm. high. $485

GLASS

VASES LALIQUE

A Lalique globular vase of matt opalescence, 16.5cm. high. $495

Lalique vase decorated with pairs of budgerigars. 24cm. high. $505

Heavy Lalique cylindrical glass vase, 22.5cm. high, 1920's. $655

A fine trial vase by Rene Lalique. $675

Spherical Lalique frosted glass vase, 25.5cm. high, 1920's. $720

Lalique opalescent glass vase of beaker form, 18cm. high, engraved France.$720

A Lalique vase of flared trumpet shape, 21cm. high. $790

Lalique frosted glass vase, 15cm., 1920's. $1,070

Lalique opalescent Ceylan vase, 1925, 9½in. high.$1,070

LALIQUE

Bulbous Lalique glass vase, 24.75cm. high, 1920's.
$1,080

Lalique vase of duodecagonal section, sided with applied cicada handles, 22.5cm. high.
$1,125

Lalique globular vase, 10in. diam. $1,135

A superb vase by Rene Lalique, circa 1925.
$1,730

Lalique turquoise glass vase, 25.25cm. high, circa 1920. $2,080

Good Lalique 'grasshopper' vase, 27cm. high, 1920's.
$2,475

Lalique frosted glass vase, 24.75cm. high, 1920's.
$3,600

A superb Lalique vase with a border of bacchantes. $6,750

Lalique amber glass serpent vase, 1930's, 24.5cm. high.
$10,125

215

GLASS

VASES
LEGRAS

Legras etched and internally decorated glass vase, 39cm. high, 1920's. $200

A Legras cameo glass vase of quatrefoil shape, the frosted glass body overlaid in purple, 13cm. high. $340

Legras cameo glass vase, circa 1900, 24.5cm. high. $700

LOETZ

Loetz iridescent glass vase, 14.25cm. high, circa 1900. $325

Loetz iridescent vase, circa 1900, 27.5cm. high. $390

Loetz iridescent glass vase, 18.5cm. high, circa 1900. $415

Loetz iridescent glass vase, 12.5cm. high, circa 1900. $540

Attractive Loetz iridescent glass vase, circa 1900, 17cm. high. $610

Loetz iridescent glass vase, circa 1900, 21.5cm. high. $630

216

LOETZ

VASES

Loetz type sterling overlay vase with blue iridescent glass, circa 1900, 7in. high. $650

Loetz iridescent glass vase, circa 1900, 7.75cm. high. $665

Loetz iridescent glass vase, 15.75cm. high, circa 1900. $830

Good Loetz iridescent glass vase, 17.5cm. high, circa 1900. $890

A Loetz glass bottle vase with a blue base decorated with flame designs. $1,325

Good Loetz iridescent glass vase, circa 1900, 12.5cm. high. $1,350

Loetz iridescent glass vase, circa 1900, 20cm. high. $1,525

Iridescent glass vase by Loetz, circa 1900, 30.75cm. high. $1,690

Good Loetz iridescent glass 'rosewater sprinkler', 24cm. high, circa 1900. $2,475

GLASS

VASES
MOUNT WASHINGTON

Late 19th century Mount Washington decorated Jack-in-the-Pulpit vase, New Bedford. $200

Burmese glass vase, labeled Mount Washington Glass Co., circa 1890, 11¾in. high. $1,150

Rare Mount Washington peachblow vase with scalloped rim, New England, circa 1890, 4¼in. high. $2,500

MULLER FRERES

Muller Freres cameo glass vase, circa 1900, 19.5cm. high. $540

Muller Freres cameo glass vase, 12.25cm. high, circa 1900. $525

Muller Freres carved cameo glass vase, circa 1890, 18.5cm. high. $945

Art Deco vase in pate de verre, signed Muller Freres. $1,175

Muller Freres carved cameo glass vase, 1890's, 40cm. high. $1,533

Large Muller Freres cameo glass landscape vase, circa 1900, 55cm. high. $1,690

GLASS

German clear glass vase in a silver plated pewter case by Orivit. $55

Early 20th century Wave Crest opalene glass vase by C.F. Monroe Co., Meriden, Connecticut. $90

Moser iridescent glass vase in graded mulberry tinged with pink. $100

One of a pair of Mary Gregory cranberry glass vases, 5ins. tall. $100

Signed Sabino vase, circa 1920, with fish motif, 8in. high. $170

Coralene and Rubina glass vase with flared neck, late 19th century, America, 7¾in. high. $200

French engraved glass vase, base marked Escalier de Cristal Paris, 28cm. high, 1870's. $255

Clutha glass vase in olive green with white and blue striations, circa 1895. $270

American gold iridescent Art glass vase, signed Aurene 729, circa 1900. $300

GLASS

VASES NAMED

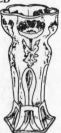

Etched and gilded vase in Orivit gilt metal mount, circa 1900, 25.75cm. high. $315

Tall French enameled vase, circa 1900, 48cm. high. $330

One of a pair of Georg Adam Scheid plique-a-jour vases, 13.75cm. high, circa 1900. $415

Small 18th century Sang-de-Boeuf bottle, 4¾in. high. $420

Durand flared-form Art glass vase, signed, with gold feather decoration, 30cm. high. $425

A Pilkington Royal Lancastrian vase designed by Walter Crane. $430

De Vez glass landscape vase, circa 1900-10, 22.25cm. high. $475

Good gilt and enameled Marcel Goupy vase, 24.5cm. high, 1920's. $485

Richardsen overlaid glass vase, 11in. high. $485

Cristallerie de Pantin cameo glass vase, circa 1900, 16.5cm. high. $495

Le verre Francais cameo glass vase, 1920's, 47.5cm. high. $495

Durand blue iridescent glass vase, 18.8cm. high, circa 1910. $520

Clutha vase designed by Christopher Dresser, of flat shape, 39.4cm. high. $530

Le verre Francais-Charder cameo glass vase, 1920's, 35cm. high. $540

French cameo glass vase, signed De Vez, circa 1905, 7¾in. high. $550

Good Lobmeyr 'Islamic' enameled vase, 13.6cm. high, 1870's. $575

A Pilkington lustre vase painted with a continuous pattern of rampant griffins, scrolls and flowers in cobalt blue and gold. $665

Degue overlaid and etched glass vase, 1920's, 40.5cm. high. $675

221

GLASS

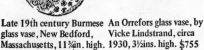

Late 19th century Burmese glass vase, New Bedford, Massachusetts, 11¾in. high. $750

An Orrefors glass vase, by Vicke Lindstrand, circa 1930, 3½ins. high. $755

German blue overlay vase by F. Zach, circa 1857, 22cm. high. $790

A Brocard enameled cylindrical vase with stylised cornflower sprays, 16.5cm. high. $855

Early 19th century American footed Hawkes cut glass vase, 20in. high. $900

'Bulle de Savon' opaline ormolu mounted two-handled vase with waisted neck, circa 1830, 16.5cm. $935

Eugene Rousseau glass vase, circa 1885, in shaded bubble brown glass, 18cm. high. $945

J. F. Christy oviform vase designed by Richard Redgrave, 1847, 15cm. high. $945

One of a pair of American Libbey amberina Art glass vases, circa 1900, 9in. high. $950

Edelzinn pewter mounted vase, circa 1900, 25cm. high. $1,015

Clutha glass vase attributed to Christopher Dresser, circa 1885, 51.7cm. high. $1,025

Austrian iridescent glass vase by Koloman Moser, circa 1900, 29cm. high. $1,035

Double-handled glass vase, by W. Northwood, 1883, 33cm. high.$1,035

Baccarat millefiori small vase, 3¾in. high, with star cut base. $1,080

Very rare Staffordshire opaque white enameled glass vase, 5in. high, circa 1760. $1,080

Unusual carved and internally decorated Christian glass vase, 1890's, 15.25cm. high. $1,170

One of four Swiss 19th century baluster vases in glass with silver gilt mounts, 3½in. high, by Bossard, Lausanne.$1,450

A good heavy art deco glass vase, by Andre Thuret, 1930. $1,510

VASES
NAMED

A pate de crystal vase by Francois Emille Decorchemont, circa 1927. $1,620

Blue baluster vase, gilt in the atelier of James Giles, circa 1765, 21cm. high. $1,650

Blue aurene decorated vase by Steuben Glass Works, Corning, New York, circa 1905, 6¾in. high. $1,700

One of a pair of Egermann Lithyalin ormolu mounted oviform vases with slender flared necks, circa 1834, 43cm. high. $2,880

Facon de Venise 'verre a serpents' of 17th century Netherlandish origin. $4,365

Pate de cristal vase by Francois Decorchemont in deep blue glass, 25.5cm. high, circa 1910. $9,000

One of a pair of green tinted vases and covers by James Giles, 16in. high, circa 1765. $13,500

14th century two-handled Syrian vase of glass, enameled in colors, 30.5cm. high. $16,875

Early wood and metal mounted Bakalowits glass vase, 1900, 46.5cm. high. $21,375

PEKIN

Unusual translucent white Pekin glass vase, carved with landscape panels and two pink dragons, 21.2cm. high. $430

Attractive turquoise Pekin glass vase of compressed pear shape, 27.5cm. high. $450

Pekin overlay glass vase of bottle form from the Qianlong period. $620

Unusual overlay Pekin glass vase of baluster form, clear metal cased in transparent green, 28cm. high.

ST. LOUIS $1,800

Well carved Imperial yellow Pekin glass vase of beaker form carved with blossom, 20.5cm. high.$1,915

18th century Pekin glass vase of clear olive green, 5½in. high.$4,725

One of a pair of St. Louis overlay Macedoine vases, bowl with waved rims, 14cm. high. $365

St. Louis shot glass vase, 11cm. high. $2,025

One of a fine pair of French mid 19th century Cristalleries de St. Louis vases with 'crown' paperweight bases, 25.7cm. high. $7,590

GLASS

VASES
STEVENS & WILLIAMS

Stevens & Williams cameo oviform vase, 7½in. high. $640

Stevens & Williams 'silveria' oviform vase with everted ogee rim, circa 1890, 23.5cm. high. $1,440

Stevens & Williams two-color cameo glass vase, circa 1900, labeled, 14in. high. $3,800

STOURBRIDGE

Stevens & Williams cameo vase of pale amber ground, with Stourbridge Art Glass marks, circa 1890, 11.5cm. high. $450

Stourbridge cameo glass vase, 5in. high, central band with turquoise Jeweling' $1,530

Late 19th century vase attributed to Joshua Hodgetts, Stourbridge, white on amethyst glass, 27.5cm. high. $12,150

TIFFANY

Tiffany iridescent glass vase, 9.5cm. high, 1912. $385

Free-form Art glass vase, by Tiffany, on dome foot, 26cm. high. $500

Tiffany trumpet-shaped glass vase on domed foot, 37.5cm. high. $650

TIFFANY

VASES

A Tiffany Favrile turquoise iridescent vase with ovi-form body, 13.5cm. high. $970

Late 19th century Tiffany Favrile gold iridescent vase, New York, with rolled neck, 6¾in. high. $1,150

Tiffany flower form vase with green and white flower, 11¾in. high. $1,530

A Tiffany Cypriot vase. $2,250

Tiffany iridescent glass vase, 18cm. high, 1914. $2,310

Tiffany iridescent glass soli-fleur vase, 35.25cm. high, 1907. $2,925

Tiffany flower vase of milky tone, 44cm. high. $4,050

Gold and yellow iridescent vase by Louis C. Tiffany, 38cm. high, circa 1900. $6,075

A rare Jack-in-the-Pulpit Tiffany peacock iridescent glass vase, 1900. $11,250

VASES
WEBB

19th century English deep yellow blown vase by Webb, 8½in. high. $150

Finely engraved Webb's glass vase, 12in. high. $260

A Webb yellow and white satin glass vase. $675

A Webb glass cameo vase, 9ins. high. $755

Rare early 20th century Webb 'rock crystal' engraved vase by Wm. Fritsche, 25cm. high. $945

Cameo glass vase by Thos. Webb & Sons, 10.8cm. high. $925

Webb 'ivory cameo' glass vase with tall neck, 31.7cm. high, 1880's. $945

Webb ruby cameo glass vase, dated 1895, overlaid in white, 13.2cm. high. $1,210

Late 19th century Webb cameo glass vase, 9.5cm. high. $1,295

A fine white and blue
Webb cameo vase.
$1,350

Thos. Webb cameo oviform
vase by George Woodall,
circa 1880, 21cm. high.
$1,350

A Webb white and blue
cameo vase, 6in. tall.
$1,620

Webb cameo glass vase in
pink and white overlay.
$1,970

Unsigned Webb two-color
cameo glass vase, circa
1900, 7¾in. high. $2,800

A superb Thomas
Webb vase. $3,330

Very rare Webb 'gem
cameo' vase in mid-blue
overlaid with white, 1889,
25.4cm. high.$6,290

Very rare Thomas Webb
cameo glass vase and cover in
amethyst overlaid in white,
circa 1885, 29.5cm. high.
$10,650

Webb three-color cameo
glass vase. $12,940

GLASS

VASES
WOODHALL

Cameo glass vase by George Woodhall, 8in. high.$6,600

George Woodhall cameo glass vase, 12ins. high, with kingfisher blue ground. $29,450

Cameo glass vase by George Woodall, 1885. $42,750

WATER GLASSES

Engraved composite stemmed water glass, circa 1745, 14cm. high. $230

Engraved water glass with flared bowl, engraved with a border of arabesques, circa 1750, 13cm. high. $290

Engraved water glass of drawn trumpet shape, circa 1758, 15.5cm. high. $840

WINE COOLERS

One of a set of seven Victorian glass wine coolers, 14cm. diam. $80

Mid 19th century Bristol clear glass wine cooler with characteristic prismatic cutting round the neck. $145

A gilded blue tulip design wine cooler signed by Isaac and Lazarus.$900

GLASS

WINDOWS

Victorian stained glass leaded light window, 2ft. 4in. tall. **$150**

Large, 20th century, stained glass window depicting a ship in full sail. **$150**

19th century stained glass window of a Saint. **$175**

Late 18th century architectural lunette window, 94in. long. **$850**

Early 20th century stained glass window depicting a peacock, 22in. high. **$200**

One of a set of three Victorian stained glass windows, 63in. high. **$1,250**

A triptych stained glass thistle window by Tiffany, circa 1904, 36in. wide. **$2,475**

Large Scottish school leaded stained glass window, circa 1900, 290cm. high. **$3,585**

A triptych stained glass landscape window, circa 1905. **$3,635**

WINE GLASSES

Victorian ruby wine glass with clear glass stem. $15

German Royal commemorative glass, engraved with a horseman. $55

18th century wine glass, the molded bowl with engraved border, 5¾ins. high. $90

Rare opaque twist wine glass with drawn trumpet bowl, 1770, 17.1cm. high. $90

A wine glass with half molded funnel bowl, on a multi-spiral and gauze opaque twist stem. $90

Wine glass with conical bowl, circa 1740, 6in. high. $95

18th century cotton twist stem glass. $100

18th century wine glass with diamond stem and engraved bowl. $110

Late 18th century air twist stem glass. $110

GLASS

Soda glass with bell bowl on air twist stem and plain foot, circa 1760. $115

Mercury-twist wine glass with pan-topped bowl, stem with two entwined spirals, circa 1750, 16.5cm. high. $120

An opaque twist wine glass. $120

Opaque twist wine glass with deep ogee bowl, 1770, 16.2cm. high. $125

Facet stem wine glass with round ogee bowl, diamond cut stem and plain foot, 1780, 15.8cm. high. $125

Engraved wine glass, circa 1740, 6in. high. $130

Airtwist wine glass of slender waisted bucket bowl, circa 1750, 18.5cm. high. $135

An opaque twist wine glass with floral decoration to the bowl. $145

Incised-twist stem wine glass with flared bowl, circa 1750, 6in. high. $145

233

WINE GLASSES

18th century wine glass with an engraved bowl. $145

Opaque twist wine glass with flared funnel bowl set on a double series opaque twist stem on a high conical plain foot, 1770, 13.8cm. high. $145

Opaque twist wine glass with funnel bowl, 1760, 15.4cm. high. $145

Opaque twist wine glass with medium-size bucket bowl, 1760, 16.5cm. high. $145

Rare late 19th century unsigned Dorflinger two-color cut-glass wine glass, Eastern United States, 4½in. high. $150

Wine glass with wide bell bowl on a stem with single mercury corkscrew, 7in. high, circa 1750. $155

Opaque twist wine glass with pan top bowl flared at the rim, 1770, 14.6cm. high. $160

18th century wine glass with funnel bowl and air twist stem. $160

Balustroid wine glass with trumpet bowl, circa 1730, 17cm. high. $160

Wine glass with flared bucket bowl on double-knopped multi-spiral air twist stem, circa 1750, 6in. high. $165

Pink twist wine glass, circa 1760, 6½in. high. $165

Late 17th century Netherlandish small wine glass, 4½in. high. $170

Faceted wine glass with slightly flared ogee bowl and a petal cut and scalloped foot, 1770, 15.2cm. high. $180

Wine glass with funnel bowl, vertically molded and ladder ribbed to its full height, 1770, 15.2cm. high. $180

Light baluster wine glass with flared funnel bowl, circa 1740, 16cm. high. $185

Wine glass with pan-topped bowl on a multi-spiral air twist stem, circa 1750, 6¾in. high. $190

Wine glass with flared 'tulip' bowl, 1760, 16.5cm. high. $195

Engraved balustroid wine glass, bell bowl with a border of fruiting vine, circa 1735, 17cm. high. $195

235

WINE GLASSES

Engraved wine or cordial glass, circa 1750, 6¼in. high. $200

Color twist wine glass with ogee bowl, circa 1770, 14.5cm. high. $205

Small baluster wine glass with funnel bowl, circa 1715, 12cm. high. $215

Balustroid wine glass, bowl of drawn trumpet shape, circa 1740, 18cm. high. $215

An excise wine glass with a round funnel bowl engraved with a sprig of fruiting vine, 6¼ins. high, circa 1745. $215

Balustroid wine glass with bell bowl supported on a short plain section, circa 1730, 16.5cm. high. $215

Unusual wine glass, 6in. high, circa 1720. $225

Composite stemmed wine glass, bowl set on a double-stem, circa 1750, 17cm. high. $230

Early liqueur glass with bell bowl on folded conical foot, 5in. high, circa 1730. $235

Early engraved wine glass.
$235

Composite stemmed wine
glass with bell bowl, circa
1750, 17cm. high.
$240

Air twist wine glass of
Jacobite significance,
circa 1750, 15cm. high.
$240

Light baluster wine glass
of Newcastle type, circa
1750, 16.5cm. high.
$255

Engraved wine glass
with ogee bowl,
circa 1760, 6in. high.
$260

Wine glass with bucket
bowl, circa 1750, 6in.
high. $260

Mercury-twist wine glass of
drawn trumpet shape, circa
1750, 17cm. high. $260

Airtwist wine glass with
bell bowl, stem with an
applied vermicular col-
lar, circa 1750, 16cm.
high. $270

Baluster wine glass, gene-
rous bell bowl set on a
drop knop, circa 1720,
19cm. high. $270

237

WINE GLASSES

Kit-Kat wine glass of drawn trumpet shape, circa 1745, 17.5cm. high. $285

Lynn opaque twist wine glass, funnel bowl with horizontal ribs and stem with a gauze core, circa 1765, 16.5cm. high. $290

Wine glass of drawn trumpet shape, on folded foot, circa 1740, 17.5cm. high. $290

Wine glass with a bell bowl set above a mixed twist stem, circa 1760. $290

Baluster wine glass with funnel bowl, inverted stem with base knop, circa 1700, 12cm. high. $290

Engraved opaque twist wine glass of Jacobite significance, circa 1770, 15.5cm. high. $295

Wine glass with cup-shaped bowl, circa 1750, 5¼in. high. $295

Wine glass with ogee bowl, circa 1750, 6¾in. high. $295

Facet stemmed wine glass, with ogee bowl, cut in the style of James Giles, circa 1780, 15cm. high. $300

GLASS

WINE GLASSES

Wine glass vertically molded funnel bowl decorated with eight panels, 1750, 15.8cm. high. $305

Jacobite air twist wine glass, funnel bowl, engraved with a sunflower, circa 1750, 15cm. high. $310

Jacobite opaque twist wine glass, bucket bowl engraved with a rose and a bud, circa 1770, 16cm. high. $310

Mixed twist wine glass with a waisted bell bowl, 1755, 18.7cm. high.$325

Engraved mixed twist wine glass, 1760, 15.2cm. high. $325

Mid 18th century opaque twist wine glass. $325

Opaque twist wine glass with plain ogee bowl set on vertically drawn opaque stem, 1760, 15.8cm. high. $325

Late 19th century Eastern United States two-color cut-glass wine glass, 4½in. high. $325

Baluster wine glass with bell bowl, 7¼in. high, circa 1730. $335

239

GLASS

WINE GLASSES

Airtwist wine glass, funnel bowl on a double-knopped stem filled with spirals, circa 1750, 17.5cm. high. $335

Composite stemmed wine glass of drawn trumpet shape, stem with beaded baluster knop, circa 1750, 18cm. high. $350

Wine glass with unsual double ogee bowl with molded vertical ribs, 5¾in. high, circa 1750. $360

Engraved light baluster wine glass with funnel bowl, 6½in. high. $365

Tartan twist wine glass with a bell bowl, stem with an opaque corkscrew core, circa 1770, 16cm. high. $370

Fine, large gilt wine glass, circa 1760, 7½in. high. $370

Kit-Kat wine glass, 6½in. high, circa 1730. $385

Baluster wine glass with a bell bowl, stem with a triple annulated knop, circa 1715, 16.5cm. high. $390

Composite stemmed wine glass in four parts, circa 1750, 6½in. high. $395

240

Lynn wine glass, the ogee bowl with five horizontal rings, 1760, 13.6cm. high. $395

Unusual wine glass, 6in. high, circa 1760. $405

Facet stemmed engraved wine glass with ogee bowl, circa 1780, 15.5cm. high. $405

Color twist wine glass with bell Bowl, circa 1770, 16.5cm. high. $425

Engraved facet-stemmed wine glass with funnel bowl, circa 1780, 16cm. high. $430

Light baluster stem wine glass with a domed and folded foot. $450

Anglo-Venetian wine glass, funnel bowl with gadrooned lower part, circa 1690, 14cm. high. $465

'Captain' glass with large ogee bowl supported on a heavy double series opaque stem, 1760, 17.2cm. high. $470

Incised twist bright emerald green wine glass on incised stem and foot to match, 1750, 13.3cm. high. $470

WINE GLASSES

Wine glass, circa 1725, with four-sided shouldered tapering stem. $475

Sporting opaque twist wine glass with ogee bowl, circa 1770, 15cm. high. $480

Facet-stemmed Jacobite wine glass with funnel bowl, circa 1780, 15cm. high. $480

Mixed twist wine glass with waisted bucket bowl, circa 1760, 17cm. high. $485

Newcastle wine glass, circa 1750, 8½in. high, with bell bowl. $495

Dutch engraved glass with thistle bowl on a knopped stem, circa 1750, 18.5cm. high. $500

Air twist Jacobite wine glass with bell bowl engraved with a rose and a bud, circa 1750, 16.5cm. high. $530

Composite stemmed wine glass of three parts, circa 1750, 7¼in. high. $540

Bohemian enameled wine glass, circa 1745, 6½in. high. $540

GLASS

Dutch engraved wine glass with thistle-shaped bowl, lower part cut with arched and faceted flutes, circa 1760, 19.5cm. high. $545

Rare mixed twist Jacobite wine glass with bell bowl, circa 1760, 17.5cm. high. $545

Engraved composite stemmed wine glass with bell bowl, circa 1760, 16.5cm. high. $550

Rare engraved opaque twist wine glass with octagonal ogee bowl, circa 1765, 15cm. high. $570

A wine glass engraved with flowers, apples and pears. $575

Heavy baluster wine glass, bell bowl supported on a knop above a slender drop knop, circa 1710, 17cm. high. $580

Unusual Lynn wine glass, 5¾in. high, circa 1750. $610

Jacobite wine glass with air twist stem, circa 1750, 5¾in. high. $625

Opaque twist wine glass, gilded, with ogee bowl, 1770, 14.6 cm. $630

243

GLASS

WINE GLASSES

Anglo-Venetian wine glass, circa 1700, 5½in. high, with conical bowl.
$640

Jacobite air twist wine glass with pan-topped bowl, circa 1750, 15.5cm. high. $645

An ogee bowl wine glass with color twist stem, 5¾in. high, circa 1770. $650

Engraved Hanoverian wine glass, 6½in. high, circa 1740. $675

Unusual pedestal stemmed wine glass with bell bowl, circa 1730, 18.5cm. high. $690

Engraved color twist wine glass in the Jacobite taste, circa 1770, 14.5cm. high. $690

Baluster wine glass with round funnel bowl, circa 1720, 7in. high. $715

An engraved color twist wine glass on a white lace twist stem, surrounded by two translucent green spirals, 7¼in. high. $720

Rare bright olive green wine glass, the rim of which is heavily gilded, 1750, 16.5cm. $720

Green wine glass with double ogee bowl, circa 1760, 15cm. high. $735

Baluster wine glass supported on triple annulated knop terminating on a domed foot, circa 1715, 15cm. high. $760

Engraved air twist wine glass of drawn trumpet shape, circa 1750, 17cm. high. $800

17th century Facon de Venise wine glass, 6¼in. high. $810

Color twist wine glass, 6½in. high, circa 1750. $810

Double-flint wine glass, 7in. high, circa 1700. $845

Dutch Royal engraved wine glass with flared bowl, 17.5cm. high, circa 1740. $855

Opaque twist wine glass with inscribed bowl, circa 1765, 18cm. high. $960

Baluster wine glass, circa 1730, 6½in. high. $965

GLASS

WINE GLASSES

Color twist wine glass, 5¾in. high, circa 1760. $965

17th century Netherlandish Façon de Venise wine glass, 6½in. high. $965

German white glass enameled in color, 15cm. high. $970

Very rare wine glass, circa 1740, 7½in. high. $990

Cut and engraved wine glass, circa 1780, 6in. high. $990

Multi-knopped air twist wine glass, circa 1750, 6¼in. high. $1,000

17th century Venetian wine glass with waisted bowl on a hollow cigar-shaped stem, 20.5cm. high. $1,070

17th century Façon de Venise wine glass with round bowl on a ribbed knob stem, 12.5cm. high. $1,070

A magnificent wine glass with a conical bowl, solid at the base and set on a four sided Silesian stem, circa 1715. $1,080

246

GLASS

An early wine glass, the waisted trumpet bowl set in a stem of colored and opaque twist. $1,080

Early 18th century wine glass with single tear. $1,150

Engraved color twist wine glass with bell bowl, circa 1770, 18cm. high.
$1,370

A rare pan topped color twist wine glass, the stem containing a central red brick thread surrounded by two opaque white spirals, 5¾ins. high.$1,440

Very rare wine glass with trumpet bowl on bobbin stem, 7¾in. high, circa 1730. $1,530

Tartan twist wine glass, circa 1760, 6½in. high.
$1,530

Color twist wine glass with pan-topped bowl, circa 1770, 14.5cm. high.
$1,550

An 18th century coin glass, with a bell-shaped bowl above a hollow knop containing a George III threepenny piece circa 1762, 6¾ins. high:$1,730

Engraved color twist wine glass, 7in. high, circa 1760.
$1,935

247

WINE GLASSES

Engraved friendship glass, probably by Jacob Sang, 7¾in. high, circa 1750. $1,950

Dutch engraved whaling glass, 7¼in. high, circa 1750. $2,025

Rare gilt and enameled armorial wine glass, circa 1730, 6in. high. $2,080

Facon de Venise winged wine glass, Low Countries, 17th century, 18cm. high. $2,925

An 18th century Amen glass with the crowned monogram of the Pretender James III of England and VIII of Scotland and underneath the word Amen, (repaired foot).$3,170

Canary twist wine glass with hammer molded bowl, circa 1760, 6in. high. $4,950

Stipple-engraved wine glass, by David Wolff, circa 1770, 6¼in. high. $5,950

Rare Jacobite wine glass engraved with badge of Society of Sea Sergeants. $6,105

18th century English wine glass etched in diamond point with Jacobite verses, 15.9cm. high. $8,910

INDEX

249

250

POCKET-SIZE IDENTIFICATION AND
PRICE GUIDES TO FOUR CATEGORIES
OF POPULAR COLLECTIBLES

THE LYLE ANTIQUES & THEIR VALUES

GLASS • FURNITURE
SILVER • CHINA

*Each book contains over
2,000 black-and-white illustrations.*

Compiled and designed by the staff of *The Lyle Official
Antiques Review*, each of these handy volumes includes
up-to-the-minute prices for over 2,000 items. With de-
tailed illustrations and precise descriptions, they provide
dealers, collectors, and buyers with basic information on
a broadly representative selection of specialized antiques.
Pocket-size and bound in a flexible cloth binding, perfect
for use in shops, flea markets, and at auctions, *The Lyle
Antiques and Their Values* are your keys to smart antique
buying. $5.95 each.

At your bookstore or order from Department LAV, Coward,
McCann & Geoghegan, 200 Madison Avenue, New York, NY
10016. Please add $1.60 for postage and handling to each order
and state and local taxes where they apply. A complete list of all
Lyle publications on antiques and of other books for collectors
of antiques is available from Coward, McCann & Geoghegan
upon request.